T0316686

Cambridge Elements ☰

Elements in the Philosophy of Immanuel Kant
edited by
Desmond Hogan
Princeton University
Howard Williams
University of Cardiff
Allen Wood
Indiana University

KANT ON CIVIL SOCIETY AND WELFARE

Sarah Holtman
University of Minnesota

CAMBRIDGE
UNIVERSITY PRESS

CAMBRIDGE
UNIVERSITY PRESS

University Printing House, Cambridge CB2 8BS, United Kingdom

One Liberty Plaza, 20th Floor, New York, NY 10006, USA

477 Williamstown Road, Port Melbourne, VIC 3207, Australia

314–321, 3rd Floor, Plot 3, Splendor Forum, Jasola District Centre,
New Delhi – 110025, India

79 Anson Road, #06–04/06, Singapore 079906

Cambridge University Press is part of the University of Cambridge.

It furthers the University's mission by disseminating knowledge in the pursuit of
education, learning, and research at the highest international levels of excellence.

www.cambridge.org
Information on this title: www.cambridge.org/9781108438742
DOI: 10.1017/9781108529747

First published 2018

A catalogue record for this publication is available from the British Library.

ISBN 978-1-108-43874-2 Paperback
ISSN 2397-9461 (online)
ISSN 2514-3824 (print)

Kant on Civil Society and Welfare

Elements in the Philosophy of Immanuel Kant

DOI: 10.1017/9781108529747
First published online: 24 October 2018

Sarah Holtman
University of Minnesota

Abstract: What justifies state-sponsored supports for individual welfare within a Kantian political system, as well as the purpose and extent of such supports and the form they may take, are vexed questions. This Element characterizes and assesses main contenders (including minimalist and middle-ground accounts) by examining the competing interpretations of Kant's larger political theory that found their social welfare claims. It then develops and defends an alternative based in civic respect. This emphasizes the perspective and institutional commitments Kant's model of citizenship entails and what is required to respect each as both a person and a participant in joint governance.

Keywords: Kant's political theory, justice, innate right, social welfare, citizenship

ISBNs: 9781108438742 (PB), 9781108529747 (OC)
ISSNs: 2397-9461 (online), 2514-3824 (print)

Contents

1 Introduction

1.1 Competing Interpretations of Kant

The extent of civil society's obligations to provide for the welfare of citizens and others, to employ its laws and institutions to offer what I term *state-sponsored social welfare*, is notoriously controversial. At one end of the spectrum is a minimalism that relegates welfare-related matters, among them provision for basic needs including food, shelter and education, to the realm of charity. At the other are accounts embracing provision for basic needs, and more, as obligations of justice. (Articles 25 and 26 of the Universal Declaration of Human Rights [1950], for example, respectively recognize universal rights both to "a standard of living adequate for the health and well-being" of oneself and one's family and to education "directed to the full development of the human personality.")

Interpretations of Immanuel Kant's work on justice, welfare and the state reflect this range of views. The early twentieth-century work of Hermann Cohen and Karl Vorländer suggests, for example, that Kant's ethics grounds a critique of capitalism and, indeed, a form of socialism. Writing a century later, Allen Wood contends that "Kantian right would sooner result in a social democratic state than in [one] friendly to wealth and privilege" (Wood, 2014, p. 84). Interpreters including Mary Gregor, and more recently B. Sharon Byrd and Joachim Hruschka, by contrast, see Kant as a minimalist where state powers are concerned. As they understand it, the Kantian state's primary functions are enforcement of contracts and protection of citizens' rights of personal security and property from violation through force or fraud. On this view, positive state action in support of individual welfare is justified only to the extent required to serve these central aims under current conditions. Where welfare-related laws and institutions are justified at all, it typically will be with an eye to preserving the state itself.

As in the more general debate, there also are Kant scholars who adopt a middle ground. Agreeing that Kantian justice primarily addresses issues of force and fraud, they nevertheless reject the conclusion that this warrants a characterization of the Kantian state that excludes or severely curtails its welfare-related efforts. Allen Rosen, for instance, understands Kant's state as a proper vehicle for addressing widely shared individual needs through benevolence. Though his account rejects state benevolence, Arthur Ripstein both accepts a similarly limited interpretation of Kantian justice at its core and rejects the claim that this necessarily leads to a minimalism that eschews state-sponsored social welfare. Under circumstances including those in which most now live, he argues, adequate support for essentially purposive citizens (those for whom force, fraud and the violation of valid contractual agreements are foundational threats) may include access to state-sponsored health care or similar benefits associated with the welfare state.

Due in part to worries that justice with too extensive a reach may make unreasonably burdensome demands, Onora O'Neill's Kantianism would provide space for welfare-related state actions based in virtue rather than justice. Yet she also emphasizes that many apparently benign societal practices in fact are problematically coercive. They thus require state intervention on behalf of those economically or otherwise burdened that aims, most fundamentally, to address force and fraud in the name of justice. Neither these middle-ground philosophers, nor those who posit a far more significant role for the Kantian state in social welfare, claim that Kant explicitly, or even implicitly, discusses the kinds of state programs they endorse. Reading his works more expansively than some will allow, each rather argues for Kant-based extensions applicable to issues and conditions Kant does not address and did not envision.

We might suspect that the explanation for such disparate interpretations lies in Kant's texts, which some characterize as at least sufficiently ambiguous to encourage such readings and perhaps so indeterminate that competing and wide-ranging interpretations in fact fit them equally well. Certainly Kant's *Metaphysics of Morals*, comprising both his most fully developed views on political philosophy (in Part I, the *Rechtslehre* or *Doctrine of Right*) and his account of moral virtue (in Part II, the *Tugendlehre* or *Doctrine of Virtue*), is notoriously difficult to read. This is especially true of his discussion of the nature and purpose of the just state in the *Rechtslehre*.

There is good reason to think, though, that the explanation for interpretive diversity does not lie principally in the *Rechtslehre*'s vexed language, or even in some special difficulty that plagues the passages on poverty relief and other welfare-related issues. As I suggest in the sections that follow, we can trace it instead to varying understandings of Kant's larger projects in moral and political philosophy. In particular, it reflects contrasting interpretations of his views on the purpose of the state, his characterization of citizenship and his understanding of the relationship between justice and virtue.

Toward that aim, this introductory section begins with a brief overview of the general concept of social welfare and of elements of Kant's practical philosophy potentially relevant in determining its place within the laws and policies of the just state Kant envisions. It further highlights central and relatively uncontroversial aspects of Kant's account of justice relevant to understanding and evaluating the discussions that follow. To the extent possible, we should start with a clear idea of the concept, of its potential connections with political theory as Kant conceives it and of the texts likely relevant to any decisive argument.

Subsequent sections address the main interpretive divisions just described. Focusing in each case on several central proponents, these discussions detail and analyze not only the characterizations of state-sponsored social welfare on offer but also the interpretation of underlying Kantian moral and political theory thought to support each proponent's position. Thus Section 2 takes up the minimalist interpretation, concentrating on views that Mary Gregor first outlines and that Byrd and Hruschka later embrace and extend. It closes with a brief discussion of F. A. Hayek's Kant-influenced views. Section 3 considers accounts that likewise understand Kant's state as foremost concerned to prevent force and fraud, but that also offer grounds for expanding the reach of state-based Kantian welfare well beyond what minimalists would endorse. The focus here is on the particularly influential readings that Rosen, Ripstein and O'Neill offer.

Accounts rejecting the force-and-fraud model as too narrow to capture Kant's conception of the state, and thus of social welfare, are my focus in Section 4. Rather than seeing Kantian justice as most fundamentally committed to preventing specific ills, these emphasize substantive and process-oriented connections between justice as Kant sees it and interrelated notions of agency, reciprocity and the general will. The resulting characterizations of social welfare are at once more fully integrated with Kant's texts and more robust in the welfare supports they endorse than minimalist and middle-ground alternatives. While several examples (especially work by Allen Wood, Paul Guyer and Howard Williams) give a fuller sense of the landscape, central here is my own reading of Kant as what I term a *civic respect* theorist. Ultimately more true to Kant's aims and concerns than the force-and-fraud model, this civic respect interpretation takes Kant's characterization of citizenship as central to justice as he understands it. The view emphasizes, in particular, the perspective and institutional commitments Kant's model of citizenship entails and what is required, from this standpoint, if we are to respect one another both as fellow participants in projects of joint governance and as individual persons. This focus on citizenship, and on just governance as a project we undertake together, places Kant's conception of those who receive social welfare supports and those responsible for providing them at the forefront. In so doing, it directly engages those whose lives and relationships are most centrally at issue and positions us especially well to grasp what is required to realize justice as Kant understands it in the face of social welfare concerns. Focusing on domestic poverty relief and foreign aid to child victims of disaster, I close this section with examples of the civic respect approach at work both at home and abroad.

1.2 Kantian Starting Points

1.2.1 State-Sponsored Social Welfare: Overview of Issues

Before we consider Kant's views in any detail, an overview of the issues regularly in play in discussions of state-sponsored social welfare is in order.[1] Beyond questions concerning the extent of such supports are ones addressing their ground or justification, the needs or interests at which they aim, appropriate recipients and whether we gauge success by appeal to outcomes for individuals or groups. Answers to these questions, of course, are not completely separable. Moreover, the accounts we consider in later sections often do not address them all, at least not explicitly. It is nevertheless worth identifying questions like these at the start so that we have the range of relevant issues firmly in mind. This will help us appreciate not only where the views under discussion differ, but what ground they share and to what extent.

As we have seen, whether in the Kantian realm or more broadly, proponents offer varied bases for understanding states as bound by social welfare obligations or empowered to address social welfare concerns. Moral grounds commonly include obligations of justice, or of moral virtue or some combination of the two. Some authors instead see the state's social welfare activity as wholly or partly determined by more pragmatic questions. Perhaps, for example, the extent to which a state addresses social welfare issues should depend on what is necessary to ensure its own continued existence (e.g., by preventing mass exodus, revolution or a severe breakdown in respect for state laws and institutions).

Again, as our brief characterization of Kant-related views already suggests, those addressing questions of state-sponsored social welfare often are concerned not only with the extent of and grounds for state actions but, relatedly, with the needs or interests these should or could seek to address. Is the state's aim (founded in justice, virtue or practicality) to prevent anarchy or dissolution, to offer minimum protections against force and fraud and facilitate private cooperative agreements, to support individual development and success in realizing ends by providing for agency-related needs, to secure happiness, to fulfill obligations of beneficence or something else?

As for appropriate recipients, debates concern whether we best understand these to include all citizens, all who find themselves within state borders, also

---

[1] All citations to Kant's texts, including *The Groundwork of the Metaphysics of Morals* (G), *The Metaphysics of Morals* (MM), "On the Common Saying, That May Be Correct in Theory, But It Is of No Use in Practice" (TP) and *Towards Perpetual Peace* (TPP), use the volume and page number of the German Academy edition of *Kants gessammelte Schriften*, ed. the Royal Prussian Academy of Sciences (Walter de Gruyter, 1900–). Quotations are from Kant (1996) translated by Mary Gregor.

needy others who are neither citizens nor residents, or perhaps only those in any or all of these groups who meet certain further qualifications (e.g., that they are law-abiding or capable of producing something of value to the society as a whole). Regarding what I described as criteria for success, options familiarly (though not exclusively) include whether supports adequate to meet aims are reasonably available to each individual or, instead, whether some measure of group benefit is as great as possible given relevant circumstances, even if some enjoy nothing or in fact suffer losses.

1.2.2 Some Central Points of Kantian Agreement

1.2.2.1 Justice, Happiness and State Purpose

Despite the deep differences just highlighted, Kant's interpreters find consensus at some crucial junctures. In particular, there is wide agreement that the central purpose of the state, as Kant conceives it, is not to promote happiness, whether of citizens or others. The state instead functions foremost as a vehicle for securing justice (or right).[2] The demands of justice, moreover, are neither coextensive with nor reducible to what supports or secures such happiness. They are instead founded in a conception of individual freedom and properly given voice through fixed or stable standards applicable to each individual falling within their scope.

Passages in the *Rechtslehre* and elsewhere drive this point home:

> [T]he concept of external right as such proceeds entirely from the concept of freedom in the external relation of people to one another and has nothing at all to do with the end that all of them naturally have (their aim of happiness) and with the prescribing of means for attaining it. (TP 8: 289)

> With respect to [happiness] no universally valid principle for laws can be given. For both the circumstances of the times and the highly conflicting but always changing illusion in which someone places his happiness (though no one can prescribe to him in what he can place it) make any fixed principle impossible and [happiness] in itself unfit to be a principle of legislation. (TP 8: 298)

> The concept of right, insofar as it is related to an obligation corresponding to it (i.e., the moral concept of right) . . . does not signify the relation of one's choice to the mere wish (also the mere need) of the other, as in actions of beneficence or callousness, but only a relation to the other's *choice*. (MM 6: 230)

> By the well-being of a state must not be understood the *welfare* of its citizens and their *happiness* . . . By the well-being of a state is understood, instead,

---

[2] I typically render the German *Recht* as "justice." This seems apt wherever Kant is characterizing standards to which domestic and international laws and institutions must conform in order to satisfy requirements of moral legitimacy.

that condition in which its constitution conforms most fully to principles of right; it is that condition which reason, *by a categorical imperative*, makes it obligatory for us to strive after. (MM 6: 318)

Full interpretation of these passages requires a close look at surrounding theory (a project for later sections). Even cursory examination, though, warrants some uncontroversial conclusions. First, the special task of the Kantian state, indeed its moral obligation, is to address issues of justice and closely related questions of individual freedom through legislative functions (and executive and judicial ones as well). As a conceptual matter, moreover, justice first and foremost concerns the choices individuals make, and individuals' capacity to make them. Its foundational focus is not on needs or desires, nor is its aim to render individuals happy, satisfied or contented.

As Kant understands it here, promoting happiness demands a focus on what is required to produce a sentiment or feeling rather than on what is necessary to honor or support individual choice and action. Moreover, as Kant often observes in earlier work in moral philosophy, the sources of happiness or satisfaction vary from person to person and even from time to time with respect to the same person. In this, happiness also diverges from the concept of justice as Kant characterizes it. For the demands of justice do not vary with individual desire or sentiment. Finally, on Kant's view there is a difference between the welfare of a state and the satisfaction or happiness of its people. The state fares well when it succeeds in its defining task, in securing justice for the citizenry through the enactment of laws and their subsequent interpretation and execution. But to say that the state successfully accomplishes this task is not to say that it satisfies the desires of the individual members of its population, or even of a certain portion or percentage of these. Nor is it true that persons within the just state necessarily will enjoy a sense of satisfaction or comfort. Doing justice is conceptually different from making people happy in any of these senses, and empirically speaking there is no guarantee justice and happiness will go hand in hand. All of this means, of course, that in the discussions that follow we have to understand securing social welfare as something more than or distinct from simply securing individual happiness, at least insofar as we see it as an aim or obligation of the Kantian state.

It is also important to the task at hand, to acknowledge what the previously cited passages do not say or imply, at least not clearly. First, nothing here rules out the possibility that the demands of Kantian justice and supports for individual happiness or well-being are indeed importantly connected in some way. Still less do these passages support the conclusion that legislation ensuring access to basic goods (nourishment, shelter, education and medical care, for example) cannot be matters of justice on Kant's account, or on a reasonable extension of it. For both happiness generally and foundational supports for individual welfare may be essential to meaningful use of liberty and property rights, civic participation and other matters typically numbered among central concerns of justice. In particular, they may be crucial to the sense of security, self-respect and hope for future success that help form the foundation for development, evaluation and implementation of one's choices. Finally, to the extent that these matters are essential to the meaningful realization of justice, they are essential to the welfare of the state as Kant conceives it and not merely to that of citizens and others residing within it. In short, though further textual analysis is certainly required, nothing in these well-known and frequently cited passages rules out happiness or well-being, even quite broadly conceived, as an appropriate or even necessary subject of state legislation on a Kantian model. Provided we can establish their connection to yet-to-be analyzed conceptions of justice and freedom, such matters may significantly shape laws and institutions in the Kantian state.[3]

1.2.2.2 Divisions in Kant's Practical Philosophy

Beyond the potentially complicated relationship between justice and happiness, we must also keep in mind the well-accepted view that the realms of justice and virtue are, for Kant, importantly distinct. As a general matter, many who question the state's role in addressing social welfare concerns instead characterize these as the province of moral virtue, and many adherents (minimalists and otherwise) accept this as the best understanding of Kant's theory as well. Further, the conceptual distinctions between justice and virtue on Kant's account may suggest that standards of virtue are structurally suited to addressing social welfare issues in a way that those of justice are not. This provides a further reason to mark the distinction now for more careful examination in what follows.

As mentioned, Kant divides his *Metaphysics of Morals* into two elements, one developing an account of justice and the other an account of moral virtue. As some passages divorce considerations of happiness from the realm of justice on conceptual grounds, others mark a sharp conceptual division between justice and virtue. Kant makes it a point, first, to distinguish the demands of justice and those of morality or "ethics" more generally (which include those of virtue). He does so by addressing, for each, the relevance of a person's reasons or motivations in acting:

---

[3] For discussion of the historical setting in which Kant makes his remarks on individual happiness and welfare that is in harmony with these distinctions see Kaufman (1999), ch. 2.

> [I]t cannot be required that this principle [of universal right] be itself in turn
> my maxim, that is, it cannot be required that *I make it the maxim* of my
> action; for anyone can be free so long as I do not impair his freedom by my
> *external action*, even though I am quite indifferent to his freedom or would
> like in my heart to infringe upon it. That I make it my maxim to act rightly is
> a demand that ethics makes on me. (MM 6: 231)

In other words, although in Kant's view the morality of an action famously
depends not only on its conformity with moral principle but also on whether it
is done "from duty" (i.e., *because* this is what morality demands), the same
requirement does not apply to evaluations of justice. The justice of one's action,
says Kant, depends only on its conformity with the principled demands of
justice. A person's reasons for so acting are simply beside the point for such an
evaluation. This distinguishes requirements of justice from those of moral
virtue in particular, Kant emphasizes in the *Tugendlehre*, because of the
relationship between justice and external coercion. Taken generally, on
Kant's view moral requirements carry a demand for moral motivation with
them. By contrast, the notion of "strict right" or justice, analyzed on its own
without reference to moral connections, is not only consistent with but includes
the possibility of external coercion as one ground or reason for compliance.
Thus,

> as right generally has as its object only what is external in actions, so strict
> right, namely that which is not mingled with anything ethical, requires only
> external grounds for determining choice; for only then is it pure and not
> mixed with any precepts of virtue. (MM 6: 232)

A second central difference between the demands of justice and those of
moral virtue, in particular, brings into play interrelated considerations that we
might best term *rigidity* and *context sensitivity*. A well-known *Tugendlehre*
discussion remarks on this difference. Duties of virtue, Kant tells us, are "of
wide obligation," and those of justice are "of narrow obligation" (MM 6: 390).
Most evidently, this claim concerns the rigidity of relevant standards. Standards
of virtue allow for a "playroom" or flexibility. For in this realm, "the law cannot
specify precisely in what way one is to act and how much one is to do by the
action for an end that is also a duty" (MM 6: 390).

Determining precisely what Kant means by this requires further analysis, of
course. For present purposes, though, two things seem clear. First, standards of
virtue acknowledge that there are some moral requirements one can fulfill
without giving voice to moral principle on every occasion that presents the
opportunity to do so. Thus, to take a common example, we can properly deem
a person beneficent although she does not act on every available opportunity to

benefit others. Second, duties of virtue are also wide in the sense that they admit of different levels of action. To continue the example, they allow for varying degrees of beneficence or aid to others on those occasions where one provides it. Kant adds that some duties of virtue are narrower than others in these respects. Nevertheless, as a class they differ from those of justice. Standards of justice require that actions conform to them whenever applicable, and this conformity leaves little room if any for variation. Justice demands that we do or refrain from some action, and we must do what is required, full stop.

The remaining difference between these standards that we consider here at the start follows from this discussion of width. What permits variations in the realm of virtue, it seems, is something about the context at hand. The comparative flexibility of standards of virtue does not give one free rein to do as one pleases. Especially, one cannot make exceptions to moral demands. Wide duty instead gives us "permission to limit one maxim of duty by another (e.g., love of one's neighbor by love of one's parents)" (MM 6: 390). To this extent, duties of virtue are sensitive to the interplay between moral principle and worldly circumstances and happenings, for instance to the fact that today is my mother's birthday or the day on which I typically stop by to have dinner with her. These standards acknowledge that I may properly take such conditions into account in determining how and when to fulfill at least some of my obligations. Standards of justice, Kant seems to indicate, are not similarly context sensitive.

These differences between justice and virtue are important background for our discussion, in part, because they offer us insight into the nature of justice and so into the role of the state as Kant sees it. At least as significant, differences between standards of justice and virtue may introduce doubts both as to whether the Kantian state has the authority to address matters of social welfare and whether, in any case, the laws and institutions at its disposal would be capable of doing so effectively. If we determine that issues of social welfare fit better under the rubric of Kantian virtue than that of justice, for example, questions arise about whether and to what extent they can be the proper province of the just state as Kant envisions it. And if we most appropriately and effectively address social welfare issues through noncoercive, flexible and context-sensitive standards, the laws of the just state might be a poor vehicle for achieving these aims.[4]

---

[4] Section 4 addresses the flexibility and context-sensitivity properly belonging to Kantian justice. They are, I argue, the very sort that due attention to social welfare requires.

1.2.3 Basic Elements of Kant's Theory of Justice

The principal explanation for varying understandings of the relationship between justice and state-sponsored social welfare on Kant's view, I suggested earlier, lies in the widely varying interpretations of his theory of justice itself. The main sources of these differences – or controversies – become clear as we consider interpretive details. Beyond the broad topics of agreement just considered, though, there also are other fixed points. A grasp of these relatively uncontroversial elements of Kant's theoretic framework is essential for understanding and evaluating both the interpretations to come and the differences among them.

1.2.3.1   The Nature of Justice

Kant's *Rechtslehre* account of justice begins by distinguishing "positive Right," the past or current laws of a particular state, from his own topic, those laws and actions that conform to universal standards of justice (MM 6: 229). The first, of course, is a matter for empirical inquiry. The second demands reason-based analysis focused not on what the current laws are, but on universal standards that can and should serve those who seek to develop, evaluate or reform such laws.

Mentioned briefly earlier, the conceptual analysis of universal (rather than positive) justice that Kant offers next is presumably central to this inquiry. Conceptually, recall, considerations of justice only arise in Kant's view where one person's choices and actions can affect another's, and all proper questions of justice concern this relationship. This helps to explain why neither motivations that give rise to an action, nor the likelihood that the action will bring another happiness or satisfaction, is justice-relevant. Questions of justice concern a choosing actor's ability to influence another's choices and the actions that give them voice. Expanding on our earlier discussion, then, we can understand that Kantian justice simply is "the sum of the conditions under which the choice of one can be united with the choice of another in accordance with a universal law of freedom" (MM 6: 230). The first (or universal) principle of justice, which Kant apparently intends as a kind of summation of this analysis, provides that:

> Any action is right if it can coexist with everyone's freedom in accordance with a universal law, or if on its maxim the freedom of choice of each can coexist with everyone's freedom in accordance with a universal law. (MM 6: 230)

As we have seen, on Kant's view, a person whose action or condition satisfies this principle acts justly no matter her reasons or motivations in doing so.

Anyone who hinders this person, moreover, wrongs her. According to Kant, such a hindrance cannot "coexist with freedom in accordance with a universal law" (MM 6: 231) and thus violates the principle of justice. The phrase "a universal law," it seems, signals that true standards of justice are both applicable to and the same for all persons. Given that questions of motivation do not arise in determining the justice of actions, Kant restates his universal principle in the form of a law that is, again, equally binding on and protective of all:

> [S]o act externally that the free use of your choice can coexist with the freedom of everyone in accordance with a universal law. (MM 6: 231)

Likewise by all accounts central to Kant's analysis is his discussion of the earlier-noted relationship between justice and coercion. As Kant defines it in "On the Common Saying, That May Be Correct in Theory, But It Is of No Use in Practice" ("Theory and Practice"), and again in the *Rechtslehre*, coercion is "any limitation of freedom through another's choice" (TP 8: 290). Coercion that impedes a just action is unjust on Kant's analysis, but when offered to oppose injustice, such a "hindrance or resistance to freedom" (MM 6: 231) is itself just. Divorced from morality more broadly speaking, justice in its purest sense therefore requires coercive motivations for its dictates. Whatever their other features, then, state laws that conform to justice will be coercive. They will, e.g., provide state backing for the enforcement of valid sales and contracts, seek to influence the choices and actions of those contemplating criminal undertakings like theft or unjustified physical violence, and offer protections for any other individual rights that state laws recognize and justice sanctions.

1.2.3.2 Innate Right, Citizenship and the General Will

Further elements central in presenting the framework of Kantian justice are the account of what Kant terms the *innate right of freedom*, the requirement that individuals join the state and the characterizations of citizenship and the general will. As described thus far, justice has no particular content. We can understand the concept but know little if anything about what actions justice sanctions or prohibits beyond the fact that it equally protects the free choice and action of each. There is considerable disagreement about exactly how to understand what more Kant tells us on this score, but certainly there is more. In particular, although the content of the specific rights and limitations that individuals enjoy or shoulder awaits further specification, there is on Kant's view one right that is innate, or common to all persons simply in virtue of their humanity. This right is "freedom" (MM 6: 237). Described most generally it is, unsurprisingly, "independence from being constrained by another's choice" to the extent that this independence "can coexist with the freedom of every other in accordance with a universal law" (MM 6: 237).

One might be tempted to conclude, given this language, that innate freedom tells us no more than we knew before about the substance of justice according to Kant. In fact, though, he follows this general account of right with a much richer analysis:

> This principle of innate freedom already involves the following authorizations, which are not really distinct from it (as if they were members of the division of some higher concept of a right): innate *equality*, that is, independence from being bound by others to more than one can in turn bind them; hence a man's quality of being *his own master* (*sui juris*) as well as being a man *beyond reproach* (*iusti*), since before he performs any act affecting rights he has done no wrong to anyone; and finally, his being authorized to do to others anything that does not in itself diminish what is theirs. (MM 6: 238–239)

Freedom as Kant understands it, then, is not an undifferentiated whole, but rather includes several elements: 1) "innate equality"; 2) the quality of being one's "own master" (or *sui juris*); 3) the quality of being "beyond reproach" (*iust[us]*); and 4) authorization "to do to others anything that does not in itself diminish what is theirs" (MM 6: 238–239). There is wide agreement that this analysis offers insight into the substance of justice on Kant's view, thus into the requirements positive state laws must satisfy. There is far less agreement, though, as to precisely what that guidance is. Thus many take the passage, together with others, as clear evidence that the founding aims of justice concern force, fraud and contracts freely made; others (myself included) read it to support a rich conception of civic personhood that founds more substantial state obligations.

Despite this marked disagreement, interpreters concur that, for Kant, insurmountable hurdles thwart individual attempts to exercise innate freedom ourselves and to respect it in others in the absence of a state comprising legislative, judicial and executive institutions. Central among these hurdles, they further agree, are concerns to solve issues of security and under-determination without unduly limiting individual self-governance. They likewise accept that, as Kant sees it, we should understand the lawmaking authority that successfully achieves this aim as embodying the "united will of the people." As Kant puts it, "only the concurring and united will of all, insofar as each decides the same thing for all and all for each, and so only the general united will of the people, can be legislative" (MM 6: 314). So conceived, coercive legislation can regulate conduct to provide security through just standards applicable to each while also respecting every citizen as a free, equal and independent legislator

(MM 6: 314). The attributes of citizens "united for giving law" are "lawful *freedom* … civil *equality* [and] civil *independence*" (MM 6: 314).

Importantly, Kant's thought here is not (most agree) that the state's morally legitimate laws are ones to which all citizens, or at least a majority, have in fact assented via some democratic voting procedure. Although a citizenry might legislate in this way, Kant instead has in mind that what legislative legitimacy requires at the level of laws themselves is hypothetical consent. The coercive laws a state rightly may apply and enforce are those that the citizenry, viewed as free, equal and independent members, would enact to govern all members including themselves. Such laws thus likewise acknowledge each as appropriately held responsible for conforming her chosen actions to just standards. As Kant makes clear in *Toward Perpetual Peace*, he believes it is a republican system that, over time, will yield a just set of laws that is likewise rightly interpreted and enforced. In such a system, it appears, legislators are citizens' democratically elected representatives.[5] At least in theory, though, laws with quite different origins, e.g., those of an unelected monarch, could be equally satisfactory from the perspective of justice. There is thus no dispute that, at least in idea, Kant's citizen is a lawmaker who participates in the united will in the sense just described and is free, equal, independent and responsible for her chosen actions (a characterization recalling the analysis of innate right).

In light of the discussions that follow, it is also worth noting that most interpreters see the innate right to freedom as (in some sense) rooted in the foundational moral theory Kant enunciates in the *Groundwork of the Metaphysics of Morals*. This is unsurprising given the right's content and Kant's assertion that it is one each properly claims by virtue of humanity. In light of the wide-ranging readings of Kant's political theory on offer, it should also be unsurprising that there is little agreement about either the locus of the connection in Kant's moral theory or the nature of the relationship between the moral theory and the political.

Some interpreters see the root of innate right in the formula of humanity, which requires that we respect the humanity in every person (including ourselves) by treating each as an end in herself rather than a mere means to other ends (G 4: 428–429). Others look to the formula of autonomy's command to respect every rational agent as possessing "a will that makes universal law" (G 4: 431). Some (myself included) appeal to the related formula of the kingdom of ends, which requires that we act only on maxims (or principles of action) that we could legislate as laws universally applicable in a community in which each member is appropriately understood as free, autonomous and

---

[5] On Kant's account of republican government see Kleingeld (2013).

equal because possessed of equal dignity or incomparable worth (G 4: 433–436). As to the relationship between *Rechtslehre* and *Groundwork* standards, some hold that innate right and the related universal principle of justice derive from Kant's moral philosophy. Others describe a much looser relationship, often citing Kant's sharp division between justice and ethics as the chief ground for doing so. In most cases, though, interpreters suggest that some appeal to the moral theory is warranted both for understanding and for extending Kant's theory of justice.[6]

1.2.3.3   Private Right

To these accounts of citizenship and state purpose, Kant adds a characterization and discussion of private right, a realm of justice that encompasses matters of ownership, or "mine and thine," broadly conceived. Together with conflicting understandings of innate right (which shape more nuanced and controversial discussions of state purpose and citizenship), those of private right are responsible for some of the starkest differences among interpreters. We can summarize what little agreement there is regarding Kant's treatment quite succinctly. In these approximately sixty pages (which are Part I of the *Rechtslehre*), Kant addresses ownership of matters external to one's person, often referring to relevant issues as arising in the state of nature. Central topics include the nature of private ownership generally and the concepts of private property and contract, as well as the rights individuals may acquire to or through them. To these subjects, commonly found in treatments of justice in the enlightenment era, Kant adds what he terms "domestic right." Here he addresses the powers and claims attending marital, parent-child and master-servant relations. A final topic under the "private right" heading concerns those acquisitions that are dependent on, or shaped by, decisions of public courts.

Here agreement among interpreters ends. As we see in the sections that follow, some read Kant's discussion to recognize just property claims that precede the state, determine its purpose and limit its authority in various ways, state provision for individual welfare among them. Some instead understand the analysis of private right as a general reflection on the scope of justice. So viewed it properly shapes our assessment of the purpose of the state and the nature of those whose interests it protects and whose actions it regulates. It does not commit Kant to the view that individuals enter the state with preexisting ownership rights or to conclusions founded on this position. Here, justice's scope may limit or shape the state's authority to attend to social welfare

---

[6] Among those rejecting interpretations that claim significant connections between Kant's moral and political theories are Willaschek (1997) and Pogge (2002).

concerns, but foundational obligations to protect preestablished ownership claims do not limit or subvert state authority in this realm. Finally, some read Kant's discussion of private right as entirely, or most importantly, conceptual. It is an investigation of key ideas one must grasp in order to understand the tasks just states must pursue and the limitations under which they do, and do not, operate. On these last readings (which express a view I share), the discussion of private right, to the extent that it is relevant at all, may be at least as supportive as not of a state role in the realm of individual welfare.

1.2.3.4   Justice in International Contexts

This brings us to the end of relevant areas of general agreement in the realm of domestic justice. For Kant, though, questions of justice do not end at state borders. Rather, he offers accounts both of justice among and between states (international justice) and of justice between a state or its citizens and foreign citizens (cosmopolitan justice). The implications of these elements of Kant's theory for state-sponsored social welfare have garnered less attention than related domestic issues. Nevertheless, they are central to a full consideration of Kant's views on social welfare matters, and, as in the domestic case, areas of interpretive agreement provide us a foundation for later discussion (in Section 4).

War and peace are Kant's primary concerns in addressing justice among states themselves. It is a matter of controversy whether to understand his main discussions (in *Perpetual Peace* and the *Rechtslehre*) to offer a just war theory or a set of principles designed gradually to eliminate war as a type of conflict that inevitably is unjust. Likewise controversial is the extent to which we should read Kant's theory to permit international interventions designed to prevent war or to protect foreign citizens from injustice.[7]

Several matters that are relevant as we consider expanding state-sponsored social welfare beyond domestic borders, though, are uncontroversial. The first is Kant's endorsement of republicanism (mentioned earlier in this Element) and his aspirations for its gradual maturation within nominally republican states and its development in those not yet warranting the title. The second is his account of the state itself as a species of moral person (MM 6: 343), presumably one due respect as a kind of free, equal, independent and responsible agent and possessed of moral obligations to citizens foreign and domestic and to foreign states. This understanding of the state apparently founds several of Kant's "preliminary" articles of perpetual peace. These include prohibitions on acquisition of one state by another and on one state's forcible interference "in the

---

[7] Williams (2012) offers thoughtful discussion and evaluation of competing views on these topics.

constitution and government of another" (TPP 8: 344, 346). The conception of the state as a moral person presumably also explains Kant's second definitive article, which proclaims, "the right of nations shall be based on a *federalism* of free states" (TPP 8: 354). Here Kant describes justice between and among states as realized not through integration in a single state under common laws, but through a federation or league that preserves and respects the separate legal structure of each member.[8]

Kant's treatment of justice between states or their citizens and the citizens of foreign states comes under the heading of cosmopolitan justice. Some see bright prospects for expanding Kant's discussion here to a variety of more contemporary issues; others view implications as far more limited. No one disputes, though, that Kant himself clearly enunciates only one tenet of cosmopolitan justice, his third definitive article of perpetual peace: "Cosmopolitan right shall be limited to conditions of universal *hospitality*" (TPP 8: 357). While it accords the foreign citizen only the right "not to be treated with hostility because he has arrived on the land of another" (MM 8: 358), Kant's own understanding of what hospitality involves is more expansive than one might expect. In particular, the demands of hospitality both prohibit turning a foreigner away where this will destroy her and mires in injustice those participants in colonialism who have "visited" foreign states in order to conquer them (TPP 8: 358–359). Whether this or other elements of Kant's view suggest a significant role for states in welfare-related matters beyond their borders is a matter of debate.

1.2.3.5   Summing Up

On Kant's view, most agree, coercive standards of justice properly regulate individual choices and actions to ensure that each person may equally enjoy the innate right of freedom that follows from her humanity or personality. This right, which at least resonates with central elements of Kant's moral theory, includes aspects of equality, independence, responsibility and free action and has evident implications for issues of property, broadly conceived. It is likewise a right that persons cannot effectively exercise or honor in the absence of a state. As Kant conceives it, the state we require to realize innate right is itself a species of moral person that unifies members under legislative, judicial and executive institutions and gives voice to the equality and lawmaking authority of each citizen member.

---

[8] This picture of states with a moral status akin to that of individuals surely also helps explain Kant's commitment to their gradual movement toward republicanism. Gradual progress is more likely to honor the reflective capacities and independent commitments of the state-as-agent.

2 The Minimalist Approach

2.1 The Evidence for Minimalism

On the minimalist interpretation (an interpretation I reject on several grounds in Section 4), Kantian justice focuses on preventing or countering the effects of force and fraud and on the enforcement of valid contracts. The Kantian state is a night watchman whose aim gives voice to justice so understood. Such a state, of course, has little or no connection to social welfare concerns.

Especially given the broad range of interpretations on offer, it is worth noting some main textual grounds apparently favoring a minimalist interpretation of Kant here at the outset. This is not because Kantians who advance this interpretation typically rely on all of these grounds. Indeed, some do not explicitly appeal to any of them. Still, each is in the background of minimalist views. Perhaps more importantly, moreover, references to the passages in question often come to the fore in debates concerning the extent to which those who favor state-sponsored social welfare can rightly appeal to Kantian theory for support. It is thus important to offer these aspects of Kant's texts as part of the foundation for the arguments Kantian minimalists do make, and to be prepared to examine them critically as we consider other interpretations and ask what may and may not be termed a genuinely Kantian approach to questions concerning justice, social welfare and the state.

As already noted, minimalists emphasize the prominent place Kant's account of justice gives to topics of property and contract. These lengthy discussions not only precede his account of public right, proponents point out. They seem to suggest that attention to these topics is the central purpose of the just state. Those adopting the minimalist view also understand Kant's discussion of the innate right of freedom to support their position. At base, as they see it, this is the right of each individual to set and pursue ends likely to vary widely from person to person. The state's aim is to protect this right equally in each citizen without unduly limiting anyone's pursuit of her ends. When taken together with the discussion of private right, minimalists hold, Kant's treatment of innate right suggests that he envisions, as central to the just state, protection for both a wide freedom to acquire and use private property and an expansive freedom of contract.

Minimalists often rely on several further passages to support and fill out their interpretation. These include Kant's remarks regarding the way state laws and institutions should address inheritance, voting and state-supported poverty relief. They also include his broader discussion of the relationship between commerce and cosmopolitanism. Unlike the discrete elements of Kant's texts addressed in Section 1, the interpretation of these more detailed discussions is quite controversial. So I mention the texts, and the minimalist take on them, briefly here in anticipation of further examination later on.

Two passages, both in the essay "Theory and Practice," at least initially seem to reveal Kant's endorsement of strong protections for private property in those who have it and his advocacy of some positive relationship between property ownership and political status. The first is an element of Kant's treatment of the equality of citizens in a just state (one anticipating the related *Rechtslehre* discussion). Here Kant is adamant that laws sanctioning hereditary privilege, allowing a son to inherit his father's title and associated prerogatives, for example, are inconsistent with the demands of justice because inconsistent with appropriate recognition of citizen equality. A person's "fellow subjects," Kant proclaims, "may not stand in his way by means of a hereditary prerogative ... so as to keep him and his descendants forever beneath the rank" (TP 8: 292). Kant immediately qualifies this requirement as regards inheritance, though. For on his view, a person may pass on to his heirs "whatever is a thing (not pertaining to personality) and can be acquired as property and also alienated by him" (TP 8: 293). Moreover, one may do this, Kant holds, despite the fact that over time inheritance practices may "produce a considerable inequality of financial circumstances among the members of the commonwealth" (TP 8: 293). Together with related comments, this willingness to protect inheritance rights seems to have implications for equality of opportunity. Specifically, it seems to demonstrate a preference for those owning property.

To better understand these implications, consider the central principle of citizen equality that Kant enunciates in "Theory and Practice." This demands that each member of the commonwealth "be allowed to attain any level of rank within it ... to which his talent, his industry and his luck can take him" (TP 8: 292). Kant's observations that the way to higher rank is properly sensitive to talent, hard work and luck, including, as we have seen, the luck of materially fortunate birth, seems to many evidently to mark him as an advocate of what we often now term "formal equality of opportunity."[9] Provided there are no formal provisions limiting a person's participation in desirable social and political offices, positions and the like, the fact that material means or other products of luck, talent or effort might prevent success raises no issue of justice.[10] Those whose family, industry, general good fortune or talent provide them material advantages (education, manners, the ability to impress the already powerful with their fine taste), Kant seems to say, may use these to promote their social or

---

[9] Rawls (1971) famously distinguishes formal and fair equality of opportunity.

[10] Such limits might include, e.g., "No indigent person may be awarded a place in Harvard's freshman class" or "No person of Jewish descent may be licensed as a lawyer."

political rise without injustice. And this is a theoretical position most friendly to those who are, or may become, propertied.

The second passage often thought to support the minimalist comes close on the heels of these remarks on inheritance, speaking now to the further citizen feature of independence. Here Kant observes that, though all citizens are to be considered "free and equal under already existing public laws," this does not mean that they are also "equal with regard to the right to give these laws" (TP 8: 294). Instead, the state recognizes the freedom and equality of each, and especially the demand that coercive laws be backed by the general will, by ensuring that only those who are *sui juris* may vote (TP 8: 294–295). This in turn requires, on his view, that any qualified voter must have "some property ... that supports him" (TP 8: 295). For this assures that if a person "must acquire from others in order to live, he does so only by *alienating* what is *his* and not by giving others permission to make use of his powers" (TP 8: 295).

Kant emphasizes here that the relevant notion of property is broader than mere material possession. It includes "any art, craft, fine art or science" (TP 8: 295). He further attempts to clarify in a footnote the distinction he has in mind, classifying the person who chops my firewood or cuts my hair, unlike the one to whom I give cloth to make garments for me or hair to make a wig, as unqualified to be citizens. A similar discussion in the *Rechtslehre* is more pointed. Those who are not *sui juris* are "mere associates," "underlings" or "passive parts" of the state, as opposed to "active members," because they must be "under the direction or protection of other individuals" (MM 6: 315). The state must still treat these passive citizens as free and equal "human beings who together make up a people" (MM 6: 315). Moreover, an important element of this treatment is the demand (similar to that voiced in "Theory and Practice") that state laws be such that "anyone can work his way up from this passive condition to an active one" (MM 6: 315). Nevertheless, property ownership (albeit broadly conceived) and powers to make and give effect to decisions about my own life seemingly take center stage where citizenship and especially lawmaking is concerned. Apparently the defining mark of "civil personality," it seems that a capacity for self-direction closely linked to ownership rights is at the very heart of the purpose and functioning of the just Kantian state.

Also apparently supportive of the minimalist view are *Rechtslehre* comments Kant makes regarding poverty relief. As before, this is a puzzling passage (MM 6: 325–326, section C), and one we revisit. Two references, though, have struck some as suggesting that any assistance the state provides the poor, as such, properly aims at the state's own preservation rather than theirs. Thus Kant describes laws funding such relief as founded on the supreme commander's "right to impose taxes on the people for its own preservation"

(MM 6: 326) and identifies a society founded on and reflecting the general will as one intended or designed "to maintain itself perpetually"(MM 6: 326). This seems to some to drive home the point that the just Kantian state aims principally at protecting and empowering those who have and can make productive use of private property. While the state may place poverty relief among its aims, they conclude, positive benefit to those who can claim little or no private property is only incidental.

Kant seems (at least to some) to offer a similar argument as he enunciates the principle of universal hospitality in *Perpetual Peace*. Although (as we have seen) this right of foreign citizens may place individual welfare under the auspices of justice in an international setting, we might read Kant's qualifications to suggest otherwise. Not only does he emphasize the fact that this is a right only to visit and not to enjoy citizen benefits (TPP 8: 358). Its foundation apparently lies in "the right of possession in common of the earth's surface" and the prospect, through travel, of making use of this right "for possible commerce" (TPP 8: 358). This perhaps suggests that Kant's concern is not with individual welfare, but with supporting or encouraging entrepreneurialism. Even in the context of international and cosmopolitan justice, then, trade and the ability to use one's decision-making capacities and talents for personal acquisition are at the fore in a way that seems to favor the minimalist view.

2.2 Mary Gregor: Kantian Minimalism in Outline

While Kant indeed sanctions state legislation aimed at citizen welfare, argues Mary Gregor in *Laws of Freedom*, he does so only as "a means to the preservation of civil society and so to the realization of the State's essential purpose" (Gregor, 1963, p. 36). As she sees it, this purpose is to secure citizens' outer freedom, the freedom to act as one chooses in pursuit of one's ends, limited by the same freedom in others or "consistent with freedom as a universal condition"(Gregor, 1963, p. 42). To put the point more straightforwardly, for Gregor, the right to outer freedom is "a right to acquire rights in general," with property "as the expression, *par excellence*, of acquired right" (Gregor, 1963, p. 49). Thus Gregor espouses the minimalist view that welfare-related laws on a Kantian model aim solely at the state's preservation (for example, at preventing the kind of pain and discontent that could lead to rampant disregard for the law). Linked as it is to protection of acquired rights, with property as the paradigm, her understanding of the state's purpose is likewise restricted. Social welfare measures are to preserve the state as a night watchman that protects citizens from physical violence, property violations and fraud and provides a structure for the enforcement of valid contracts where necessary. Because she offers not only an early and extended defense of the minimalist reading but also one that has importantly influenced other proponents, a close look at Gregor's work serves as a useful overview of the approach and as a helpful prelude to other versions of Kant-based minimalism.

Three elements of this account – the relationship Gregor describes between outer freedom and perfect duties to self, the import she gives to Kant's extended discussion of property rights and her emphasis on the imperfect rationality of human agents – offer insight into the foundations and implications of her view. The *Rechtslehre* account of outer freedom and the nature and purpose of the morally legitimate state, Gregor contends, is rooted most importantly in Kant's *Groundwork* account of moral obligation. It is closely tied, in particular, to his discussion of the formula of humanity and the accompanying characterization of perfect duties to self. Gregor readily acknowledges Kant's distinction between matters of right and those of morality. Where our focus is on a question of justice (or "Law" as she terms it), broader moral considerations without more constrain neither what ends we may choose nor our motivations in advancing, abandoning or limiting those ends. Provided they do not problematically implicate others' freedom, the miser, to take Gregor's example, may justly pursue his immoral, greed-based aims. Moreover, even if moved by fear of punishment or hope for his own material gain, his actions remain fully just so long as they do not violate this freedom. Nevertheless, Gregor maintains, Kant locates "the ground of juridical concepts in the notion of moral autonomy" (Gregor, 1963, p. 46). In particular, our awareness of obligations of right is founded (on Kant's view as she understands it) in our recognition of the "right of humanity in our own person" (Gregor, 1963, p. 46).

Kantian personality or humanity, Gregor emphasizes, limits free choice most fundamentally with respect to one's own person. Each of us is morally obligated to avoid using herself simply as a means for realizing the subjective ends she sets. This duty to self, Gregor contends, thus "is the first condition of all duty" because in its absence we would not be "persons or subjects of duty," could not be conscious of our position as such and could not recognize the duties to others of which this consciousness makes us aware (Gregor, 1963, p. 46). While others' rights to be treated as ends indeed are grounded in "their possession of pure practical reason," she therefore concludes, our *obligations* to these others, among them our duties of right or justice, "proceed from our own personality" (Gregor, 1963, p. 48), from our recognition of our own moral capacities. Absent this self-recognition, we could grasp and appreciate no duties to others on Kant's view because "we can recognize that we are under obligation to others only in so far as we are conscious of a categorical imperative commanding us to act in a certain way regarding them" (Gregor, 1963, p. 47). For Gregor, this consciousness is the same thing as consciousness of our personality or moral capacity.

The lengthy *Rechtslehre* account of ownership rights preceding the discussion of justice within the state applies, we know, to a wide range of issues. Together with her position on the special place of duties to self in Kant's discussion, Gregor's take on this element of Kant's theory importantly shapes her analysis of the purpose of the state and so of its relationship to social welfare. Recognition of perfect duties to self, and thus of our own moral personality, as we have seen, grounds our consciousness of moral obligations to others on Gregor's interpretation. This includes consciousness of our obligations regarding their outer freedom (or freedom of choice and action). As we recognize first in our own case and ultimately for that of others, outer freedom, "our inherent right to the use of our own person" (Gregor, 1963, p. 50), in fact is the only right each of us possesses simply in virtue of this moral personality. It is essential to its expression or realization. But consciousness of this right, Gregor continues, carries with it the consciousness of "our right to use external objects" (Gregor, 1963, p. 50). For we can only realize and give content to outer freedom on Kant's account with reference to choices we make regarding such objects. "To the mere empty form of outer freedom," she claims, "we must add its matter, objects of choice as such, and determine what follows from the universal principle of Law regarding our acts of choice exercised upon objects" (Gregor, 1963, pp. 50–51).

For Gregor, the *Groundwork* consideration of humanity as an end, which demands that a person be able to give rational consent to the way another might make use of her, already supplies the foundation for individual rights against physical violence (Gregor, 1963, p. 51). Further reflection on the connection between personality and freedom of choice and action yields recognition not only of a right of outer freedom but also of the right to property without which we cannot conceive its exercise. To appreciate the implications for state-sponsored social welfare, consideration of appropriate limitations on individual choice and action and Gregor's related account of the state's justifying purpose also are in order. Warranted limitations will be those necessary to protect the outer freedom of each consistent with a like freedom for all (Gregor, 1963, p. 57). Gregor's final assessment of the state's underlying purpose rests on the further recognition that, as imperfectly rational beings living in conditions in which the actions of one inevitably will limit those of others, we must offer each other the mutual assurance that respect for one person's rights will not rest on the sacrifice of another's. We do so by "giving over the use of force to an authority which will guarantee our possession and, in case of dispute, determine what belongs to each of us" (Gregor, 1963, p. 57), in other words by agreeing to enter into a state.

The aim or purpose of the Kantian state as Gregor sees it, then, is to secure the outer freedom that is crucial if human beings are to realize their autonomy or personality, to set and pursue their ends. More specifically, it is to ensure bodily security, appropriate limitations on property acquisition and security in property rightly acquired. These are to be interpreted from a perspective that places the claims of the individual at the forefront and reads the rights of others as an extension of her appreciation of her own.

Given this background, it seems we should understand Gregor's characterization of the state's welfare-related role in terms of what is necessary for it to offer lasting and effective protection to each citizen as such. We must further see the citizen as respected first and foremost by provision for both bodily security and security in the prospect of acquiring means to pursue and satisfy personal ends whatever they may be. Here the characterization is of the individual member of the state as capable, self-sustaining and concerned in the first instance with her own aims and only secondarily with those of others.

Presented with a collection of citizens so conceived, the state's proper focus with regard to welfare would be, as Gregor suggests, on the state itself as an organized entity for the legislation, interpretation and execution of laws designed to secure the person and property of each toward the attainment of outer freedom. Such concerns might warrant, for example, state funding for a police force and similar protective bodies, provision of state monies for legislative and judicial investigations and deliberations and state supports aimed at ensuring citizens' loyalty and obedience, though not their uncritical acceptance of state decisions. Importantly, all of these would have as their focus not the functioning of individuals as persons and citizens, but the existence and effectiveness of the state as a protector of self-sufficient but imperfectly rational, thus imperfectly just, members.

2.3 Other Minimalist Views

2.3.1 Byrd and Hruschka on the Juridical State

I have offered Gregor's interpretation under the heading of an outline or overview because the central elements of her reading reappear in other well-worked or well-known Kantian minimalist accounts. Beyond the general considerations noted in the introduction, these elements are: the characterization of the individual as an end-setter or choice-maker; the centrality of concerns with physical security and the acquisition and protection of property broadly construed; and the assumption that the individual's capacities for setting and pursuing ends are adequate to the task of maintaining her personality, or humanity, provided others' choices are restricted to an appropriate sphere.

B. Sharon Byrd and Joachim Hruschka (2010) offer the most thoroughgoing text-based view of this sort. Unlike Gregor, who roots her discussion in Kant's foundational moral theory, their focus is more centrally on the political theory viewed in its own right and presented, in its most developed form, in the *Rechtslehre*. On their reading, Kant considers three species of "public justice," ones that must be realized via public institutions available to all and that are required elements of any state adequately securing individual rights (the "juridical state"). Two of these institutions, unsurprisingly, are protective justice (the public lawgiving that protects citizens' rights) and distributive justice (the decisions of judges authorized to hear and issue final determinations when citizen disputes over rights arise). But it is the emphasis they give the remaining institution, justice in exchange or commutative justice, that places Byrd and Hruschka most squarely among minimalist interpreters. For they construe what Kant terms "justice valid among people in their mutual inter-course" (MM sect. 36, 6: 297) as a "public market" ensuring the just "exchange of external things," a market "in which free persons engage in transactions free from interventions" (Byrd and Hruschka, 2010, p. 36).

The mere existence of these three elements, of course, does not ensure a state that satisfactorily secures individual rights (and thus attends to its essential purpose) on this view. These institutions also must meet a substantive require-ment. Understood most generally, this is the requirement that limitations on individual freedom are only those necessary to ensure a like freedom for each. As Byrd and Hruschka note (predictably, given the general characterization of Kant's views discussed in Section 1), this means that state institutions may not justifiably coerce individual conduct in order to promote citizens' happiness or welfare as distinct from their freedom. On their reading, this means not only that legislative and judicial institutions must look to freedom rather than welfare so understood. Importantly, they emphasize, state restrictions on mar-ket interactions are justified *solely* to ensure equal protection for individual freedom. To better clarify this last requirement, they add in a footnote, "Kant rejects the welfare state" (Byrd and Hruschka, 2010, p. 42, n. 99).

Full appreciation of Byrd and Hruschka's reading, and their argument for it, of course, requires a firm grasp of freedom in the relevant context. On their view, the external freedom that is the subject of justice best is understood as "independence from someone else's necessitating choice" (Byrd and Hruschka, 2010, p. 78). Unsurprisingly, respect for such freedom requires that the state shape its laws to protect citizens from physical violence and coercive threats, including those that might affect property ownership and market relations. Far more controversially, the Kantian state as Byrd and Hruschka would have it must further advance freedom through "permissive laws," or "power-conferring norms."

The chief consequence of this last is that neither the institution of property itself nor particular laws regarding its acquisition or configuration awaits the approval of the law-giving Kantian state. Thus one central element of the state's role as protector of freedom, including freedom in market exchange and acquisition, is development of laws and institutions necessary to recognize and secure property rights that precede the state. These will include laws allowing for reliable use and exchange of such property (Byrd and Hruschka, 2010, p. 101). Beyond securing rights that predate it, though, the state also must protect citizen freedom through laws that answer to and facilitate citizen demands arising after its establishment. It must do so because:

> without [the necessary institutions] my freedom would be robbed of the use of its choice with respect to external objects of choice even though my choice is compatible with the free choice of all others. (Byrd and Hruschka, 2010, p. 102)

To illustrate the scope of this requirement as they understand it, the coauthors offer the example of German laws passed to permit condominium ownership in the years just following World War II. On the Kantian view, they argue, such laws did not simply provide citizens a useful or desirable addition to ownership options. Their passage was required of the state as an answer to consumer demand for affordable dwellings and to pervading financial conditions that prevented single-owner renovation of multiunit buildings. Absent laws creating the possibility of this new form of ownership, "citizens' freedom to use the buildings would have been hindered and indeed objects of their choice would have been placed beyond any possibility of use" (Byrd and Hruschka, 2010, p. 102).

A similar line of reasoning, say Byrd and Hruschka, in fact applies to each of the main elements in Kant's discussion of private right, thus also to contractual and domestic relations. Nor are issues of "mine and thine" elements of Kant's account of the just state that interpreters or those hoping to extend the theory can appropriately separate from the rest. The placement and extended nature of this discussion, together with the way in which it fits with Kant's accounts of freedom and personhood as they read them, places property at the very center of his political philosophy. Indeed, on their interpretation, persons would never need to make the transition from the state of nature to the juridical state absent these property-focused issues. It is not that property and related matters are simply one element of Kant's political theory on this view. They are its driving force. The state's central task is to facilitate the free use of property and related rights via basic protections from force and fraud and through further legislation required so that citizens can give effect to the plans they make and the aims they set for themselves. The state thus is tasked with supporting Kantian citizens as persons who make and exercise their own judgments and, in particular, "tend to their own affairs" (Byrd and Hruschka, 2010, p. 163).

It is to be expected, given this, that Byrd and Hruschka spend little or no time considering the state's welfare-related responsibilities. Clearly, on their view, it will be important for the Kantian state to maintain well-working legislative and judicial institutions as well as an effective police power. A well-functioning juridical state (to use their term) must also provide citizens with reliable means to convey their entrepreneurial plans, and more general property and contract-related aims, to those with lawmaking powers so that the state efficiently and effectively designs laws to serve these. Presumably as for Gregor, achieving state institutions of this sort may sometimes demand attention to basic citizen needs like food and shelter. Justification for expending state resources in this way, though, would again be rooted in the need to maintain a state that works well for able and self-sufficient citizens focused on the central human function of setting and pursuing individual ends. That citizens as Kant conceives them would require or should receive state support in developing as persons or in pursuing their aims seems, on this view, beside the point.

2.3.2 Hayek on the Free Market and Social Justice

Although F. A. Hayek sees it as importantly in line with Gregor's Kant (Hayek, 1976, p. 43), his work is neither Kant interpretation or even intentional Kant extension. Nevertheless, it can help highlight what is distinctive about the minimalist view.[11]

Hayek himself suggests that what marks his work as Kantian (at least in spirit) is endorsement of a "negative test of universalizability" for determining the justice of state laws. Specifically, just laws on his view "are end-independent and refer only to facts that those charged with obeying them can know or readily ascertain" (Hayek, 1976, p. 40). Rather than demanding that laws serve justice in some positive way (e.g., that they ensure access to adequate nutrition, housing or similar), Hayek's test simply imposes negative requirements concerning neutrality and accessibility. Consistent with a wide range of individual ends or commitments, and understandable and follow-able by all, such laws will be ones each can endorse.

---

[11] I discuss Hayek, then, not because he is a Kantian in more than the weakest sense, but because his work helps us highlight themes prevalent in minimalist interpretations.

With minimalists, Hayek likewise sees justice as focused on ensuring substantial freedom to pursue individual ends and the state as a vehicle for achieving justice so understood. The route states properly employ to pursue this aim, he further agrees, is protection of private property and freedom of contract from the twin threats of force and fraud. Most enlightening for our purposes, though, are two further Hayekian claims: 1) that the founding principle of justice is "treating all under the same rules" (Hayek, 1976, p. 39); and 2) that neither ill luck (Hayek, 1976, p. 74), outcomes unreflective of true merit (Hayek, 1976, p. 65) nor mere disadvantage in one's position or expectations is sufficient to establish injustice (Hayek, 1976, pp. 92–96).

Though neither of these claims is explicit in the other minimalist views we have considered, each is a version of Kantian claims (noted earlier) that seem to support the minimalist interpretation. In particular, Hayek's founding principle of justice seems to enunciate a commitment to formal equality of opportunity of the sort often attributed to Kant in light of "Theory and Practice." Hayek's discussion of luck, merit and disadvantage further recalls the staunch claim that promoting happiness is not one with serving justice (a claim our other minimalists do explicitly acknowledge). But it also evokes Kant's characterization of the proper civic response to those who find themselves dependent on others apparently through no fault of their own. For here Kant, like Hayek, seems to suggest that while these disadvantages are undeserved, they are not unjust. While the state (and fellow citizens) cannot rightly take advantage of this plight or seek to perpetuate it, justice neither requires, nor apparently permits, positive legal efforts designed to improve conditions for such individuals.

Once we have noticed these latter elements, explicit in Hayek, it is clear that they likewise influence the other minimalist views we have considered. That state laws will not vary with the status of those to whom they apply is among the background assumptions for both Gregor and Byrd and Hruschka. That the just state is not in the business of remedying ill luck or instances where outcomes and merit part company is likewise an unstated aspect of each view. This is part of what it means for justice and the state to focus on the self-sufficient actor and seek to ensure that this person's choices drive lawmaking rather than the other way around. Just as Gregor's interpretation is useful in identifying broad minimalist themes, the concrete details of Hayek's critical response to the notion of "social justice" serve to clarify minimalist implications and commitments we might otherwise have overlooked.

2.4 Minimalism in Brief Review

Reading uncontroversial elements and contested passages together to endorse a self-reliant and entrepreneurial individualism, Kant's minimalist interpreters and followers see little place for the state where social welfare is concerned. The just Kantian state, as they understand it, should devote its energies to insuring otherwise self-sufficient individuals security from force and fraud in their persons and property and to facilitating their contractual dealings. Except to the extent these are required to preserve the state itself, on this view, supports for individuals facing other challenges (e.g., material, educational or medical) in developing and pursuing their ends is outside the state's province and antithetical to its founding aim. Middle-ground theorists, we see in Section 3, reject both minimalists' assumption of self-reliance and their focus on state preservation. In Section 4, I join others in challenging the force-and-fraud model itself as well as the conclusion (shared by many middle-ground theorists) that Kant embraces a civic perspective that is claim-focused and individualist at its core.

3 Middle Grounds

As indicated at the outset, Kantian minimalists' claims regarding state-sponsored social welfare lie at one extreme of a wide spectrum of views. As with most extremes, the universe of those who fall within it is relatively small. The vast majority of interpretations of Kant's own texts, as well as Kant-based extensions, are instead what I have termed *middle grounds*. For interpretive reasons, these views share the minimalist conclusion that justice, as Kant sees it, addresses and seeks to prevent the use of force or fraud by one person against another and aims to facilitate and enforce valid contractual agreements. According to middle-ground views, these likewise are the principal aims of states as vehicles of justice and indeed ones we have good reason to endorse and develop in extended Kant-based accounts.

These views all part company with minimalism, however, on the question of the state's appropriate role in addressing issues of individual welfare. Though on varying interpretive grounds and to varying degrees, each understands Kant (and any extended Kantianism) to embrace state-sponsored social welfare with the aim of advancing the well-being of individual citizens rather than the stability and effective functioning of the state. In what follows, as promised, I address three of these views, which find support for state-sponsored welfare through divergent interpretations of Kant's texts. Unsurprisingly, each likewise offers a distinct understanding of the role such measures would play and the supports they would encompass. While I save alternative interpretations and critical comments (my own and those that others advance) for Section 4, charitable exegesis and discussion here should not be mistaken for the conclusion that competing interpretations fit Kant's texts equally well. In my view, middle-ground accounts improve on minimalism. But in embracing both the force-and-fraud model and a conception of the just state and its citizens that is either unduly self-focused or unjustifiably spare, they fail to take adequate notice of central aspects of Kant's texts. As a consequence, they offer a picture neither as theoretically coherent nor as sensitive to practical considerations and human capacities as the one Kant in fact offers.

3.1 Rosen: State-Sponsored Benevolence

Because he explicitly criticizes the account, analysis of Allen Rosen's interpretation is especially helpful in beginning to appreciate both middle-ground departures from minimalism and similarities with it. As Rosen sees it, minimalist interpreters misunderstand two aspects of Kant's theory of justice that are importantly related to his views on state-sponsored social welfare. These are the foundations Kant provides for the *Rechtslehre* discussion of state-funded poverty relief (a passage mentioned briefly in Section 2) and the scope of the just Kantian state's legislative obligations more generally.

Despite these criticisms, though, Rosen's reading of Kant has much in common with the minimalist ones we have just considered. As he understands it, Kant's first principle of justice requires, most fundamentally, that laws and institutions be designed to ensure "maximum liberty" for all (Rosen, 1993, p. 11). To assist those applying this abstract standard in pursuit of such freedom, Kant further offers "constitutional principles" of civil liberty (or civil freedom), legal equality and civil independence. Rosen finds central prohibitions on force and fraud in the "Theory and Practice" account of civil freedom. As described there, he argues, this freedom has two components. The first, an anti-paternalistic principle, enjoins that no one be forced to live in accord with another person's conception of the good. As Rosen sees it, this chiefly protects against governments based on a principle of benevolence, one that determines the nature and extent of individual rights by assessing what best serves the good or welfare of society as a whole. Such a principle cannot serve as a ground for defining or limiting rights on Rosen's reading because it makes every liberty contingent on the state's current assessment of what promotes public welfare.

Civil freedom's second component offers a positive account of reasons adequate to specify and limit individual rights. Most generally, on Rosen's reading, "each individual should be free to pursue his own happiness as long as he does not infringe the liberty of his fellow subjects to pursue their own ends" (Rosen, 1993, p. 16). Remarking that none of Kant's writings offers clear standards for determining when one person's action does unduly infringe another's "rightful liberty" (thus warranting limitation on grounds of justice), Rosen adds that Kant's view nevertheless is clear enough. For Kant, he asserts, one's action unjustly limits others' freedom when: 1) it forcibly prevents those others from exercising their liberty in ways not unduly restrictive of freedom elsewhere; or 2) it fraudulently interferes with such liberty through deception intended to effect that purpose (Rosen, 1993, pp. 16–17).

Among those freedoms Kant deems especially valuable and worthy of protection under the auspices of justice, Rosen suggests, are free expression, "liberty to compete for personal advancement in the context of a free-market economy" and the right to acquire, hold and use private property (Rosen, 1993, pp. 19–20). As for the remaining "constitutional" standards that aid us in applying the principle of justice, Rosen understands the principle of equality to require that state laws and institutions adhere to standards of formal equality of opportunity. The principle of independence, or political freedom, as he reads it describes and protects rights of political participation including that of propertied citizens to vote in elections designating legislative representatives.[12]

In sum, then, Kantian justice on Rosen's view most fundamentally protects individual liberty (especially freedom of expression and economic liberty) from interference via force and fraud. We properly achieve justice so understood through laws and institutions that meet standards of formal equality and that are developed and amended by elected representatives in a society that grants the vote to those capable of independent living (thus presumably of independent decision-making). Linking this account with Kant's claim that justice is only achievable within the laws and institutions that are the state, Rosen succinctly identifies the state's primary purpose as seeking to achieve justice so understood. In all of this, his reading parallels the minimalist one in both its self-oriented perspective and its focus on force and fraud.

The fact that this is the state's central purpose, though, does not mean that it is all the state may or should attempt on Rosen's account, and it is here that he and the minimalist part company. Rosen develops his alternative view, first, by examining the *Rechtslehre* passage on poverty relief more closely. In particular, he points out, Kant here describes the state as acquiring from the people themselves the right to impose taxes to fund such relief, now sharing a duty or obligation that was previously only theirs to fulfill (Rosen, 1993, p. 179).

As Rosen sees it, this duty must be that of benevolence, the duty to promote the permissible ends of others.[13] This seems particularly likely, he argues,

---

[12] Rosen nicely addresses problems with these limits on political participation at some length.

[13] Others, e.g., O'Neill, term this duty one of "beneficence."

because of the apparent connection between the relevant *Rechtslehre* passage and Kant's *Groundwork* analysis. This discussion famously grounds a moral duty of benevolence on the contention that we cannot will a universal law of non-assistance consistent with our rational end of ensuring the conditions required to satisfy our present and future needs (G 4: 423). As Rosen puts Kant's point, "even the wealthiest person can never be sure that future reversals of fortune may not bring him to such a pass that his needs can only be met through the aid of others" (Rosen, 1993, p. 199).

On Rosen's reading, laws of the just Kantian state are those it is possible for an "entire people" to will without any contradiction of "rationally necessary ends" (Rosen, 1993, p. 200). This is what Kant means in saying that such laws are backed by the general will. Freedom, as described earlier in this Element, is one such end; another is providing for one's own needs. As Rosen sees it, then, we best read the *Rechtslehre* discussion of poverty relief to acknowledge both the rationally necessary end of providing for one's needs and the *Groundwork*'s argument for a duty of benevolence based on universal vulnerability and dependency. Given the relationship between rationally necessary ends and dependency, the Kantian state properly, and at least partially, assumes the duty of benevolence that each of us bears to all others. It appropriately fulfills this duty through the tax contributions of the citizenry. Although relevant needs of course include the most basic ones required for an individual's survival, they do not end there. Given our existence as end-setting agents, they may extend to what Rosen terms "general well-being" (Rosen, 1993, p. 202).

In rejecting the minimalist position, Rosen understands the state to have an essential role as protector against fraud and aggression but also as facilitator of individual ends. The additional aim, essentially one of promoting others' happiness, supplements the state's foremost obligation to serve justice. Kant's state does not exist merely to prevent invasions of liberty. It may, and sometimes must, take positive steps to promote individual welfare.

As to inevitable concern that, in doing the second, state laws will unduly limit liberty in ways that violate Kant's anti-paternalism, Rosen offers several arguments. The most significant is the claim that, like the limits prohibiting criminal activity, we best understand state-supported poverty relief, and similar measures funded through taxes and grounded in the principle of benevolence, not as limiting one person's liberty to promote another's happiness. Rather, these are among the rational requirements that demarcate the contours of particular rights and liberties and allow end-setting citizens to exercise them successfully. What renders these requirements rational, it is worth noting, is the rejection (by Rosen and Rosen's Kant) of a central minimalist assumption. What most fundamentally separates Rosen's interpretation from minimalism is rejection of the view that, protected from clear cases of force and fraud and from unjustified legal restrictions, the Kantian citizen is properly viewed as self-sufficient, as able to realize aims and fulfill obligations without assistance reliably at hand.

3.2 Ripstein: Purposive Citizens

Central in understanding and extending Kantian political theory as Arthur Ripstein would have it is a firm grasp of Kant's conception of political independence, of "what it is for each person to be his or her own master rather than the servant of another" (Ripstein, 2009, p. 5). While Rosen's reading takes civil liberty as most central to Kant's account of the just state, then, Ripstein's gives pride of place to independence, or one understanding of it.

Like Rosen, Ripstein founds his interpretation in the universal principle of justice (or right) and the related examination of innate right (in which Rosen's "constitutional principles" have their roots). Viewed through these discussions, says Ripstein, we can appreciate that Kantian independence is a relational concept. One person is independent provided no other person chooses the purposes she pursues, a relationship demanding, most fundamentally, that each control her own body. Understood in this way, says Ripstein, only "use" and "injury" violate my independence. When I use a person, I commandeer her powers to advance my own purposes. Paradigm examples involve turning another's body or actions to the support of one's own aims through force or fraud, offering her no chance to decline. Injury occurs, by contrast, when I destroy another's powers, treating them as though they are mine to employ or deplete as I please (Ripstein, 2009, p. 45).

In Ripstein's view, by placing this conception of independence (or freedom from domination) at the center of his accounts of justice and the state, Kant demonstrates that to enjoy equal freedom, as he understands it, is not to be provided equal division of some good. (This is true even when the good in question is civil liberty.) Instead, it is to be free positively to determine one's own purposes rather than compelled to advance those of others. Once freedom so understood is guaranteed, it is up to the agent to employ her own means in pursuit of purposes she has independently endorsed.

This foundational discussion of independence grounds the central elements of Kant's political theory as Ripstein understands it (among them Kant's conception of justice as it relates not only to personal security, but to property, contract and status relations). It further includes Kant's views regarding matters of social welfare. Issues of property and the like, of course, take Ripstein into the realm of private right, which he understands to encompass those claims we can justify without appeal to public institutions. These include rights against use and injury of my person that follow from the innate right of humanity. But they also include those falling within the domain of acquired right, concerning matters I might use in setting or pursuing my ends that could, in principle, belong to someone other than myself (something true neither of my body nor of my capacities on a Kantian account).

For Kant, as Ripstein reads him, where it is possible to employ matters beyond one's own body or capacities in setting and pursuing one's ends, the only justification for limiting that employment would be its inconsistency with the freedom of others. This means that the possibility of acquiring property and contractual rights, as well as the marital, parental and employment rights that arise from status relationships, must in principle be available to everyone. This, of course, expands the range of possible rights violations and of just limits on independence. Where acquired rights are in play, they justifiably prevent me, e.g., from using another person's property in ways to which she has not consented or from exploiting marital or employment relationships to advance private purposes inconsistent with the terms of those relationships. These limits, but only these, are consistent with respecting the equal claim of each to freedom as purposiveness. Importantly, on Ripstein's interpretation, neither a person's desires nor her needs can ground a right to another's action or forbearance. Kantian right, as he sees it, still demands protection only from injury or use. The discussion of acquired right simply extends justly recognized claims from those involving my person to matters rightfully in my control.[14]

Although acquired rights are ones we can justify without appeal to state institutions, though, they are not ones that are realizable in their absence. Problems of unilateral action, assurance and indeterminacy prevent justified claims of acquired right where we lack institutions permitting both public authorization and enforcement of acquisitions and adjudication of disputes by publicly authorized judges.[15] Absent these, says Ripstein's Kant, the demands of freedom as non-domination mean that unilateral acquisition cannot obligate others, that we necessarily lack assurance that our respect for others' acquired rights will be reciprocated and that we are bereft of means for resolving disputes arising from indeterminacy as to acquired rights' existence and extent. Kant's solution to these problems lies in a state understood as a system of institutions for making, executing and interpreting laws. Officials authorized to act only for the public purpose of addressing these aforementioned defects carry out each function. Besides these law-related powers, none of which

---

[14] For full discussion of acquired right, see Ripstein's ch. 3.
[15] Ripstein addresses these issues at length in his ch. 6.

a private individual can possess, says Ripstein, Kant identifies additional state powers, e.g., to create public spaces like roads and to support citizens incapable of supporting themselves.

To this point, Ripstein's freedom-from-domination reading resembles minimalism not only in its support for a narrow range of state purposes but also in its foundational commitment to the conception of the individual as a plan-maker and pursuer focused first and foremost on her own case. Particularly because he is so explicit about the second, Ripstein's relatively robust account of more concrete state powers and responsibilities may seem especially surprising. A brief look at his interpretation of Kant's poverty relief passages, though, provides clarification. It also offers a basis for later criticism.

One consequence of the Kantian state's role as just described, says Ripstein, is that its institutions must "provide the background conditions in which no one will ever be a mendicant" (Ripstein, 2009, p. 286). Neither prudence nor benevolence (nor of course any commitment to equality of benefits and burdens) plays any part in this argument. Consistent with right as Ripstein interprets it, they could not. On this view, we must define unjustifiable poverty not as a lack of what one needs or desires, but rather as the kind of resource deprivation that renders sufferers impotent to set or pursue their own ends absent others' charity. (Typically on Ripstein's view this is poverty cemented in place by institutions that define and enforce property rights.) This kind of necessary reliance on charity is, for Ripstein's Kant, a paradigmatic instance of the citizen dependence that any just state must prevent.

By way of Kantian remedy for such poverty, Ripstein offers no preferred recipe. He does claim that the question to be considered is what is required to provide for citizens' "most necessary natural needs." He adds that remedy is not limited to insuring for each what is required for biological survival, but includes other support, for example publicly funded education and health care, that is designed to help prevent domination (see Ripstein, 2009, pp. 284–286). Like Rosen, then, Ripstein departs from minimalism on questions of social welfare because he sees threats to self-sufficiency to which all are vulnerable and that extend beyond the narrow, traditional understanding of force and fraud.

3.3 O'Neill: Coercive Conditions and Obligations of Virtue

Much of Onora O'Neill's well-known scholarship on justice takes the form not of Kant interpretation, but of her own Kant-based moral and political theory. For this reason, I offer her account as a last example here, one that both interprets and extends Kant's theory and also departs from related accounts in important respects. O'Neill's views are complex and her contributions (over more than thirty years) copious. So I consider only the elements of her work most relevant for present purposes (each developed over time yet central to her current thinking). These are her broad conception of coercion, her skepticism about the limitations inherent in a rights-based perspective and her advocacy of states' adoption and facilitation of virtuous ends in both domestic and international affairs. My aim is to highlight what is distinctive about O'Neill's position in a way that demonstrates sharp differences with Rosen and Ripstein but nevertheless places her among middle-ground theorists.

The Kantian approach to issues of morality and justice that O'Neill herself favors addresses what she sees as central deficiencies in various non-Kantian views. Especially, it is an approach: 1) that both individual agents and institutions can access and put to use as they seek to determine how they should proceed, morally speaking; 2) that can offer a critical perspective on current practice; and 3) that can guide actions (again whether the actor is an individual or an institution). Kantian theory offers these possibilities, on her reading, first because it is a theory of obligation designed to address and guide imperfectly rational beings (with human beings as the evident paradigm) in determining what actions they ought and ought not undertake. Second, nothing limits the theory's appeal to individual agents alone. Both agents and institutions can have identifiable basic maxims that characterize the actions they plan to undertake (or have undertaken already) and that they can assess for moral adequacy (O'Neill, 1986, ch. 7).

In asking what one should do, morally speaking, says O'Neill, the essential question is whether one's basic maxim is shareable or "could only be adopted on the assumption that others' action is not guided by it" (O'Neill, 1986, p. 134). We are morally obligated to refrain from acting on principles that others cannot share. On Kant's view, she says, these include principles of coercion and deception, each running afoul of a perfect duty of justice, and of disrespect, nonbeneficence and nondevelopment, linked to imperfect duties (e.g., of beneficence). Taken most generally, as O'Neill sees it, coercion undermines an agent's ability to choose and act, and thus to consent to another's action or reject it. Deception undermines cognitive capacities, preventing true agreement in a different way (O'Neill, 1986, p. 139).

In framing the Kantian conception of justice in terms of coercion rather than force, O'Neill may already expand the range of issues central to justice beyond what both minimalists and many middle-ground theorists intend. As she emphasizes, although we may use violence, or threat of violence, to coerce, there are many other routes open to us. Coercion, unlike mere violence, aims to get us to act or refrain from acting through an offer that the victim cannot refuse because the alternative reliably threatens "deep damage to self or identity" (O'Neill, 2000, p. 91). Others who see Kantian justice as centrally concerned with force typically will have more than physical violence in mind. Yet O'Neill's careful distinction, and her emphasis on the way that coercion undermines choice and threatens the self broadly conceived, makes the importance of taking a broader view abundantly clear. In so doing, it also places agency in general and the deep commitments of the particular agent at the foundations of Kantian justice as she sees it.[16]

Likewise a departure from accounts already considered is O'Neill's emphasis on the importance of context. In her view, what central principles of justice require of us is something we cannot determine in isolation from the circumstances in which actions are to be undertaken. Especially, whether a particular action, practice or institution runs afoul of prohibitions on coercion depends on surrounding conditions, ones whose coercive effects may further hinge on their persistence over a span of time or their interaction with other prevailing circumstances. Thus on this Kantian view we must ask about the effects of current and proposed policies and practices on agreements and relationships already undertaken and on those proposed. And the question is not simply what likely would hinder an agent's capacity under some presumed set of circumstances, but what is true given things as they are. (Conditions likely to make a difference include poverty and servile attitudes developed due to social norms.)[17] By expressly noting the relevance of institutions and conditions as well as foundations in agent choice, identity and integrity, then, O'Neill moves inquiries regarding force and fraud well beyond minimalist parameters. She also stakes out a distinctive position on Kantian fundamentals (to which we return for more detailed comparison with Rosen and Ripstein in the next section).

O'Neill's characterization of Kantian moral and political theory is also distinctive for the emphasis it places on obligations as opposed to rights. Like any theory that takes obligation as foundational, she says, Kantian theory looks at morality and justice not primarily from the perspective of rights holders with claims, but instead from that of those "agents and agencies" who bear these obligations, whether of justice or of virtue (O'Neill, 1986, p. 122). On O'Neill's view, obligation-based theories have the benefit of making the claims of rights holders and the needs of beneficiaries secondary. Of first importance is instead the identification of relevant actors, actions and reasons. For it is these that link particular persons with the deed or exercise of

---

[16] O'Neill (2000) helpfully addresses the relationship between agency and coercion at pp. 81–96.

[17] On the relevance of context to exercising coercion, thus also to identifying it, see O'Neill (2000), pp. 91–96.

restraint that morality (broadly conceived) requires of them. These theories thus speak directly to those charged with action or restraint and encourage others to think seriously, e.g., about whether and to what extent required action is possible for those who are to discharge it and what conditions might facilitate or hinder fulfillment. It also means that, on the Kantian account, similar foundations in obligation link justice and virtue. This encourages us, as individuals and especially as citizens, to consider what combination of context-sensitive obligations might best allow us to satisfy universal duties whose fulfillment protects and supports agency.[18]

As O'Neill often emphasizes, the decision at the level of practice to recognize human rights grounded in justice that we cannot hope satisfactorily to address in every case (perhaps to healthcare, education or sustenance) makes little sense from the perspective of concern for agency and may in fact do much harm. We often do better not only to rely on institutional solutions, but to frame and seek to serve more concrete obligations of virtue. In some cases we should recognize these latter as the imperfect obligations of institutions (including political ones) rather than of individuals alone (O'Neill, 2016, ch. 11).

3.4 Reflections on the Middle Ground

We know, of course, what it is that middle-ground theories generally share, an acceptance of the force-and-fraud model together with an expanded view of the state's role in combatting such ills and their consequences for individuals through social welfare supports. With examples in place, though, we are positioned both to detail shared ground more precisely and to deepen our account of differences among theories in this intermediate group.

As for what these views share, we now can see that middle-ground characterizations of Kantian citizens and their state agree in two important respects (commonalities that separate them from minimalism in one way but in another maintain a connection with it). Middle-ground views part company with minimalism in understanding persons, and thus citizens, as both more subject to shared vulnerability and more capable of recognizing that this fact has import for civic obligations and appropriate state action than minimalists will allow. For Rosen, this yields a requirement that the Kantian state address poverty and similar shared threats to citizens' exercise of civil liberty by developing benevolent laws and institutions that support individual welfare. For Ripstein, it demands, for example, a broad understanding of the natural and social circumstances (e.g., entrenched and grinding poverty) that reduce

---

[18] See O'Neill (1986) chs. 7 and 8 on the importance of combining appeals to justice and virtue in addressing issues of social welfare from a Kantian perspective.

a person to reliance on others for her most basic needs and thus undermine her capacity to set and pursue her own purposes. For O'Neill, it requires a focus on what imperils individual agency in lived circumstances. This in turn calls on the state to be alert for hidden sources of, or supports for, coercion and deception and to be ready to bring laws and institutions to bear as means of remedying such conditions in the name of justice. It also requires that citizens, as well as institutions (governmental and otherwise), be awake to what will effectively protect and support agency in the circumstances at hand and be ready to act for this aim guided by virtue as well as justice.

Further, now with minimalists or at least in harmony with their conclusions, each of these middle-ground theorists understands the state's task as undertaken either 1) from a foundation rooted in the individual's perspective on her own case; or 2) necessarily with special caution lest what we deem obligations of justice to all impose an undue burden on some. Consequently (as I argue in Section 4), these views at best fail to recognize the capacity of Kantian justice to address the complexities that can imperil agents in our world. At worst, they neglect or minimize the import of conceptions of joint responsibility, general will and citizenship essential to Kant's account.

As we have also seen, broad similarities among middle-ground views likewise overlie marked differences, both interpretive and normative. For Rosen, it is liberty that is central to persons and citizens on a Kantian model. For Ripstein, it is an independence, or freedom from domination, that both protects a person in the setting and pursuit of her own ends and respects her power to choose when and to what extent she will assist others in realizing theirs. For O'Neill, it is agency. As she understands it, this is no radical independence to set one's own course unburdened by others' plans. It is instead a realized capacity to employ powers of practical decision in evaluating moral obligations and in determining how we best can fulfill them as a set under prevailing conditions. It is also the realized capacity to bring these powers to bear in setting and pursuing one's own ends and commitments, in particular those most central to one's integrity or sense of self. This does not mean that the principles of morality and justice themselves are up to the individual, matters she can determine by her own lights while others settle on something quite different. But it is the mark of actions, policies, laws and institutions that are duly considerate of the agency of each that they are designed to involve our critical evaluation as a central element and to conform to what we *could* adopt as consistent with and supportive of agency where fully productive participation is not currently possible.

In reading and extending Kant, then, these exemplars of the middle ground agree both that minimalists are correct in correlating justice most fundamentally with protection of individuals from force and fraud and that persons' shared vulnerabilities are more extensive than minimalists suppose. At the same time, they offer disparate readings of freedom, thus also of what is at the heart of personhood and citizenship. These divergent understandings of Kantian persons in turn give rise to alternative pictures of the just (and otherwise morally virtuous) state. Here, Rosen and Ripstein seem most in agreement. Each takes the individual's appreciation and assessment of what is central to her own personhood as a starting point and works outward toward a determination of what others likewise are due. Each also reads Kant to emphasize the important role of property and a free market economy in any state that appropriately addresses personhood so conceived. In all of this each further resembles the minimalist. O'Neill by contrast takes for Kant's starting point, and her own, not the demands of one's own personhood first of all, but the point of view of the individual assessing her obligations to persons who are agents, herself among them. The significance of agency and what is respectful and supportive of it arises from this perspective. Likewise, the limited nature of Kantian justice as she sees it, and the relationship between Kantian virtue and state efforts to promote individual welfare, do not arise from a focus on the individual's rightful claims. Their source is the view that paradigmatic protections of justice are not all we require to support agency in our world but that a more extensive justice may itself imperil agency.

4 Beyond Force and Fraud

Those adopting a middle ground on the purpose of the Kantian state and its implications for social welfare obligations certainly expand the possibilities that minimalists countenance for state action in this regard. Yet middle-ground accounts nevertheless are limited in at least two ways. The first is textual. This worry applies most evidently to Rosen and Ripstein, whose individualist accounts (like those of minimalists) arguably ill fit the language of general will and cosmopolitan community that characterize Kant's political theory. Their emphasis on property ownership and market relations, again like that of minimalists, also squares poorly with Kant's texts, whose emphasis seems, as further examination shows, to be elsewhere. Neither of these concerns applies to O'Neill as I have read her. Still, because her relevant views are rooted only loosely in Kant's texts, there are questions about the extent to which we can establish a comfortable fit between these views and Kant's own language.

A second, more practical ground for dissatisfaction applies to all three theorists, and to middle-ground views generally as well as to minimalist ones. These accounts all advocate a narrow conception of Kantian justice as one that not only fits Kant's texts but is also independently attractive both morally and pragmatically. As they characterize it, the state can rightly address issues of social welfare only where they are sufficiently connected to questions of force and fraud or (for theorists like Rosen and O'Neill) to the extent that we can establish grounds for states on Kant's model to develop laws, policies and institutions based in virtue. But how well does this narrow force-and-fraud-focused account of justice fit the beings we are and the world in which we live, and how straightforwardly can it address the issues we face? As we know, middle-ground theorists reject minimalism due in large part to its unrealistic assumptions about human self-sufficiency and their belief that Kant's texts acknowledge or leave room for a more realistic understanding of persons and offer an account of the just state in harmony with it. Their attempts to bring widely recognized concerns under the umbrella of a similarly limited conception of justice, however, yield accounts that are artificially restricted in reach, unduly unimaginative in aspiration and often limited to problematically attenuated justifications for extending justice beyond minimalist boundaries.

In what follows, I consider several views that depart minimalist and middle-ground terrain for one or more of these reasons. My particular focus in later sections is on my own *civic respect* reading. Both on textual and practical grounds, I argue, views offering more integrated construals of Kant's texts and richer accounts of justice are preferable to the alternatives.

4.1 Recent Alternatives

Among those abandoning the narrow minimalist and middle-ground readings of Kantian justice, Allen Wood, Paul Guyer and Howard Williams offer interpretations differing importantly from each other in the degree to which they take Kant to depart from a force-and-fraud model and in the textual discussions to which they appeal. They thus provide a sense both of the range of textual criticisms of minimalist and middle-ground views and of the integrating themes available to support and extend alternative readings.

4.1.1 Wood

Of the three, Allen Wood's analysis casts Kantian justice most narrowly. Wood understands Kant's work as more closely aligned with social democratic theory than with views endorsing state acceptance of extant divisions of wealth and power. Nevertheless, he argues that Kant's account is less developed and less progressive than it might be. Indeed, as Wood sees it, by comparison with his contemporary J. G. Fichte, Kant's approach is "timid" or conservative (Wood, 2008, p. 204).

Like middle-ground theorists, Wood argues that the Kantian state's obligation coercively to protect citizens' external freedom (their effective ability to make and act on individual decisions) is not only consistent with but requires that the state remedy severe poverty. Potentially, it has implications for other significant privations as well. Wood acknowledges that the justification for state efforts to address social welfare concerns cannot lie in individual happiness. As he understands Kant's objections (noted earlier), such concerns are the province of ethics or virtue. To make them the subject of coercive laws would violate the sharp distinction between right and ethics. Moreover, says Wood, equality of wealth, opportunity or the like offers no better justification for state action to address social welfare concerns on a Kantian account. Passages in "Theory and Practice" accepting inequality as consistent with justice lay this possibility to rest. Civil equality restricts the hierarchies and power differentials the state may impose on its citizens but does not require equality of wealth or other goods.

For Wood, though, happiness and equality do not exhaust the possible grounds for state-sponsored social welfare. We best read Kant instead to found poverty relief (and perhaps more) on "what is a necessary condition for any human being to exercise free agency" (Wood, 2008, p. 196). One such condition, which Wood believes Kant has in mind, is the individual's physical survival. On this interpretation, laws, policies and institutions advancing social welfare aims are justified when and to the extent that they support agency by helping to secure the foundation for its exercise and development.

Given her broad account of coercive threats to agency, O'Neill's understanding of Kant bears some similarity to Wood's. Appealing both to Kant's original contract and to his exploration of "general injustice," though, Wood suggests that a reasonable interpretation of Kant's texts may implicate threats extending beyond the kind of coercion and deception that O'Neill and fellow middle-ground theorists cite. His suggestion evolves from the argument that Kantian justice in fact demands state action to alleviate poverty.

If the purpose of Kant's state is to protect the innate right to freedom in each citizen, says Wood, then we best conceive of it not merely as *permitted* to enact laws providing state-supported poverty relief, but as *required* to do so. We can capture this idea in Kantian terms by understanding the legal standards necessary to ensure the very possibility of agency in each to be ones every citizen would endorse as required elements of an acceptable legal system (Wood, 2008, p. 198). So conceived, both standards themselves and their mandated inclusion among the state's legal provisions would be backed by the general united will as the original contract requires.

In support of this reading, Wood emphasizes discussions of "general injustice" that appear both in a brief *Tugendlehre* passage and in Kant's early notes and lectures. As he interprets them, these discussions acknowledge "unintended results of free human actions," operating together, as potential sources of injustice even where no particular individual has done wrong (Wood, 2008, p. 199). Kant's own references in this regard all concern poverty. In the *Tugendlehre*, moreover, he describes this species of economic injustice as attributable to "the injustice of the government" (MM 6: 454).

As Wood sees it, this last comment suggests that it is the state's duty to remedy such poverty through its laws and institutions, providing grounds for a strongly non-minimalist reading of the passage on poverty relief. He sees essential conditions for realizing agency, and acknowledgment that justice-relevant barriers may be collective or institutional, as providing further support. The reading thus moves beyond middle-ground parameters by linking injustice to collective institutional barriers to realized agency.

As noted, Wood is skeptical about exactly how far Kant himself would be willing to take this view concerning the appropriateness of justice-based state involvement in matters of social welfare. Kant seems only too willing, after all, to accept the ways in which inheritance practices cement inequalities of wealth in place. Moreover, he fails to describe or even consider state interventions other than poverty relief that might justly and effectively alleviate general injustice.

4.1.2 Guyer

If Wood's reading suggests an expanded picture of Kantian justice in the realm of social welfare, Paul Guyer's embraces and details such a picture. Writing against the backdrop of John Rawls's two principles of justice, Guyer asks to what extent the second of these, the difference principle, and especially its first clause, is consistent with Rawls's proclaimed Kantian foundations (Guyer, 2000).[19] His conclusion appeals to a careful reading of Kant's account of the relationship between justice and private property. On Guyer's view, Kantian justice requires that the laws and institutions of the state establish and secure a system of property. This system must be fair to each member understood as a citizen with claims to equal rights of life and liberty and must provide the

---

[19] The first part of this principle places limitations on the unequal division of wealth and income, requiring that departures from an equal division be "to the greatest benefit of the least advantaged" (Rawls, 1971, p. 302).

foundation required for each to enjoy an equal and meaningful opportunity to develop and pursue happiness, or a conception of the good. Whether or not the standard of justice giving effect to this Kantian demand would perfectly mirror Rawls's difference principle, it would understand property distribution and redistribution, toward the aforementioned aims, as demands of justice.

The difficulty in squaring a requirement for this kind of state-sponsored social welfare effort with Kant's account of justice, says Guyer, arises from the anti-paternalism enunciated in "Theory and Practice." On his view, we best understand these well-known passages not only to delineate the state's founding purpose but also to protect its citizens from undue interference. The task of the just state is to protect individual freedom, not to secure happiness, and the state that oversteps these bounds reaches beyond its authority and undermines the aims that justify its existence. It dictates or at least curtails the ends citizens may set and pursue rather than protecting, and indeed maximizing, the freedom of each (Guyer, 2000, p. 264).

For Guyer, though, an understanding of Kant's anti-paternalism that rules out a principle of distributive justice attentive to each citizen's material needs is one that fails to appreciate the depth and complexity of Kant's account of justice. At the foundation of this account, Guyer acknowledges, is a grounding principle that commands protection for the maximum freedom of each consistent with an equal freedom for every other. Nevertheless, as we know, a further foundational element (contained in the sections on private right) addresses property. On Guyer's reading, which sharply contrasts with those of minimalists in particular, this discussion establishes: 1) that a genuine right to property requires a control over external matters that is not merely physical, thus making rightful property ownership dependent on the possibility of others' rational agreement; 2) that, morally speaking, a person may claim others' consent or agreement to her purported property rights only if she is willing to recognize a similar "right to control" in them; 3) that it would be irrational to deny oneself access to property as just described, thus also irrational to refuse to recognize equally advantageous property rights in others; 4) that only a state can satisfactorily meet these demands; and 5) that coercive enforcement of state laws and institutions in keeping with them is consistent with and required by foundational demands to respect the freedom of each (Guyer, 2000, pp. 279–285).

In this way Guyer ties justice in general, and the justification of state-sponsored social welfare efforts in particular, to the prospect of exercising rights of life and liberty and of developing and acting on personal ends and projects, that is of pursuing happiness. Of course, a Kantian property regime of the sort Guyer envisions would put citizens in a position to resist attempts to exploit their material disadvantage through force and fraud. But the benefits of such a system in terms of facilitating and supporting each citizen's life as an end-setting agent would go well beyond these concerns. In Guyer's view, we could approximate them especially well in the form of Rawls's difference principle.

4.1.3 Williams

Any fully satisfactory interpretation of Kant's work on justice and the distribution of wealth, as Howard Williams (2010) reads the relevant texts, must appreciate Kant's recognition of the myriad circumstances to which states must respond and the varied ways in which they rightly may do so. By comparison with Wood and Guyer, moreover, Williams sees the scope of social-welfare-oriented Kantian argument as broad. In particular, Kantianism rejects national borders as natural stopping points because we must realize domestic and international justice together. Williams agrees with both Wood and Guyer, though, that it is concern for whatever is central to agency, not force and fraud alone, that must drive our understanding of Kant's views. Like Guyer, he also sees Kant as offering the basis for an extensive set of state-sponsored welfare supports.

Central to Williams's treatment are interpretations of Kant's "supreme proprietor" and of the state as a "moral person." The supreme proprietor is "only an idea of the civil union that serves to represent in accordance with the concept of right the necessary union of the private property of everyone within the people under a general public possessor" (MM 6: 323). On Williams's reading, this idea provides us a perspective on the people or citizenry, representing it (or them) as a "legislative union" or "civil society." So understood, the people are united under laws their legislative representatives enact and have the ultimate authority to determine how the state allocates and regulates property. While a representative group, or even a monarch, may exercise this power in any actual state, authority ultimately rests with the united general will of the people (Williams, 2010, pp. 50–51).

When Kant references the right of the supreme proprietor to tax the people in order to fund poverty relief, on this reading, he is thus referencing the right of the people itself. Their obligation to support those who live in poverty derives from the fact that the common enterprise that is the state is one whose laws are backed by the general will. Such laws justifiably coerce citizen compliance because they are ones that each as a free agent would choose to govern civic relationships generally, and property relations in particular. Such laws must, as a system, offer each a genuine opportunity to develop and function as an individual and a citizen because this is what free agents, taking all seriously as such, would choose. Where lack of material means thwarts such foundational aims, the people in the guise of their representatives have a responsibility to remedy or remove these barriers (Williams, 2010, pp. 50–56).

As Kant conceives it, says Williams, a state's realization of justice is a gradual matter, something achieved only over time and in ways that vary from state to state. Necessarily a central element of this realization, though, is the accompanying attainment of perpetual peace by means of a "federation of free states" whose members together encourage and support one another toward republicanism. Kant casts the individual states that should form this federation as themselves moral persons. Although Kant does not say so expressly, as Williams sees it, this suggests both that each federation member should view itself and all others as free, equal and independent citizens and that the standards by which members agree to govern their relationship must respect each citizen-state as such. As in the domestic case, standards should be ones each reasonably could regard as backed by the general will because they are ones supportive of the development and successful employment of citizen features.

As in the domestic case, this has implications for the way states respond to inequalities of wealth. In particular, Williams suggests, each should recognize the hazard that the agency-threatening wealth inequalities of member states and their citizens will pose to the realization of republicanism both within the impoverished state and elsewhere. No state may properly interfere with, much less take over, the governance of another, and there is no one recipe for appropriate aid. Nevertheless, it is in the spirit of Kant's texts for foreign states to seek to remedy the kind of poverty that jeopardizes the agency of fellow states and their citizens. As Williams sees it, such efforts have bases in both justice and benevolence but must always, themselves, conform to standards of justice that hold between states. (We find many of these standards in the preliminary and definitive principles of *Perpetual Peace.*) To use Williams's language:

> Kantians then say 'yes' to attempting to improve the distribution of wealth worldwide from the motive of benevolence and in order to protect, improve, and expand the federation of free states, but they say 'no' to making one state the client of the other and to giving favourable material terms to one state at the expense of others. (Williams, 2010, p. 70)

4.2 The Civic Respect Account

Like those Wood, Guyer and Williams offer, my account of Kant's political theory emphasizes connections between Kantian justice and interrelated notions of agency, reciprocity and the general will. It also recognizes a significant role for state-sponsored social welfare within Kant's theory and in reasonable extensions of it. I ground appreciation of the place of social welfare in the Kantian state most fundamentally, though, neither on general injustice, on the theory of private property nor on the idea of a supreme proprietor. As noted at the outset, my focus instead is on citizenship as Kant understands it, in particular on his general characterization of the citizen, on the perspective citizens should take regarding their institutional commitments and on what is required if they are to respect one another not only as fellow participants in joint governance but also as persons. In elaborating and advocating this *civic respect* account of Kant's political theory, I sometimes note my disagreement with the views Wood, Guyer and Williams put forward. But because they are largely in harmony with my own, I look to them more often for support.

In broadest terms, the civic respect account is an interpretive approach that seeks to make sense of Kant's theory of justice as a whole (including his views on domestic, international and cosmopolitan justice and private right). It also provides a basis for extensions of the theory to more contemporary issues that Kant did not address. Sometimes it gives us reasons to conclude that a committed Kantian can, and should, reject judgments Kant in fact endorsed at the level of policy and legislation. To put this characterization of Kantian citizenship and just governance most succinctly, as citizens, we properly understand governing in the just state as a project we undertake together, mutually committed to offering equal respect and support for each member as such through the agency-essential joint products of our association. Individually and as a set, the laws and institutions of the just state, including those addressing social welfare, must express, support and advance this understanding.

For present purposes, of course, I focus on elements of Kant's theory most relevant in grasping and extending his views on state-sponsored social welfare, offering an argument for preferring an interpretation based in civic respect to minimalist and middle-ground counterparts. To this end (in Section 4.2.1), I provide and defend a rich account of Kantian citizenship, one that is participatory and sensitive to real-world conditions rather than claim-focused and idealized. A rereading of Kant's puzzling (and potentially troubling) discussion of "passive" citizenship (in Section 4.2.1.2) further founds both an account of relevant state aims or ideals and an exploration of their implications for an appropriately Kantian understanding of equal opportunity. The section closes with a discussion of the general will (in Section 4.2.1.3), filling out the conception of citizenship on offer.

In Section 4.2.2, I elaborate and further support the civic respect account as it bears on social welfare by considering the role of private right, and in particular of private property, in Kant's theory. In contrast not only to minimalists but to Rosen and Ripstein, I argue that the system Kant advocates is one that shapes the laws governing property use and acquisition with an eye to fulfilling independent demands for the just treatment of citizens.

With fundamentals in place, I return (in Section 4.2.3) to Kant's discussion of poverty relief, now seen through the lens of civic respect. Offering a reading of that passage that squares with Kant's larger theory newly interpreted, I also address and reject minimalist and benevolence-based readings. I further highlight grounds for rejecting, as indicative of Kant's position, both Ripstein's narrow focus on mendicancy and O'Neill's worries about over-extension. In the closing sections (Sections 4.2.4 and 4.2.5), I consider the social welfare implications of Kantian justice as I understand it for both domestic poverty relief and international aid efforts. In keeping with my focus on the perspective that characterizes Kantian citizens, these examples emphasize the outlook or attitude that should shape our approach to such questions on a Kantian view and explore its implications.

4.2.1 Kantian Citizenship

4.2.1.1 Kant's Characterization of Citizens

The *Rechtslehre*, we know, offers Kant's fullest theoretic discussion of citizenship, describing the citizen as a legislator for a just state.[20] In particular, it characterizes lawmaking members by delineating the perspective from which each should view decisions made in her role not as an individual developing and pursuing personal ends, but as a legislator for a political community of free, equal and independent members.

From the minimalist perspective, the Kantian citizen grasps the value of developing ends, purposes and plans by first appreciating their centrality to her own life and only secondarily recognizing that she shares this feature with others. As an otherwise self-sufficient purposive agent, she requires protection from the force or fraud others might visit on her in order to make use of her powers in developing a life and cannot justify a failure to accord those others

---

[20] Discussions in this and the next subsection draw significantly on my account of Kantian citizenship in Holtman (2014).

like restraint. From the perspective of many middle-ground views, the only flaw in this interpretation lies in underestimating human vulnerability to force and fraud and the consequent need for a state that offers some protections in the form of social welfare supports.[21]

There is certainly a reading of Kantian legislators' freedom, equality and independence that yields a picture friendly to this minimalist (and frequent middle-ground) interpretation. On this view, we define the citizen, most fundamentally, in terms of the ways others may or may not treat her. This definition provides grounds for determining what protections a just state must offer citizens. It also founds an argument rejecting at least some social welfare supports as exceeding the reach of authorized state purposes and unduly interfering with individual ends, plans and actions. From this perspective, freedom seems simply to prohibit forced compliance with laws to which the citizen has not agreed, equality only to require that each receives a fair distribution of legal benefit and burden, and independence merely to demand the absence of subordinating pressures likely to influence decision-making.

On this interpretation, Kant's account of citizenship seems to offer a legislative perspective that is both idealized in its estimation of citizen capacities and insensitive to the implications of real-world conditions. Modeling themselves on the characteristics Kant describes, legislators in existing states should enact laws and engage in other civic tasks guided by the background assumption that those to whom these decisions apply are fully possessed of defining civic features, or nearly so. They resemble the self-sufficient citizens whom minimalists envision and whom many middle-ground theorists believe we imperfectly approximate. Because it appears to focus on capacity, the demand for independence seems especially central to this model. Indeed, we might sum up the characterization of citizens so understood by saying that, in making laws and engaging in other civic pursuits, each should assume that the fellow community members she addresses are independent individuals fully capable of making and acting on judgments guided by their own practical reason and personal capacities.

Further examination, though, supports a very different picture of the Kantian citizen, one at once more dynamic and less claim focused than both minimalist and many middle-ground adherents would have it. It also reveals that neither an idealized assumption of fully realized capacities nor a demand for strict adherence come what may characterizes Kant's legislative perspective. His conception of the citizen instead urges a focus on possibilities for creatively and

---

[21] This does not characterize O'Neill, whose concerns about a broad conception of justice I critique in Subsection 4.2.3.2.

conscientiously shaping our actions in light of broad principles and a limited set of more rigid rules. We are to apply these standards, moreover, to morally imperfect and vulnerable persons in a flawed and complicated world.

Taking citizen features in the order Kant adopts, the freedom at issue on this participatory and worldly reading is not simply, or most importantly, freedom from unwarranted coercion. In Kant's words, it is instead "the attribute of obeying no other law than that to which [the citizen] has given ... consent" (MM 6: 314). Thus (as both Guyer and Williams's analyses also recognize) it is consent, not the absence of coercive force, that must be the foundation of claims regarding a citizen's obedience. We best understand freedom, then, to describe the perspective a citizen properly takes on legal obligation. Each must view herself not only as charged with adopting standards to govern both self and others as members of a political society. She must reject as illegitimate any standards lacking such agreement. The citizen is not tasked with rule compliance on one hand and promised the protection rules offer on the other. She is a rule adopter, a position she cannot meaningfully occupy unless she may also operate as a rule rejecter. Legal obligation follows only if she has the realistic prospect of playing both roles.

Kant's characterization of citizen freedom thus focuses on the active adoption of standards that ground legal obligation. Continuing this participatory theme, his account of civic equality rests on a similarly vital conception of legal standing. Here the citizen attribute as Kant describes it is that "of not recognizing" any fellow citizen as a "superior with the moral capacity" to impose legal burdens or enjoy legal benefits that a person could not herself impose or enjoy in return (MM 6: 314). Powers to acquire property, enter a binding contract and the like are ones we use in making and giving effect to decisions about how to direct our lives. The equality in question, then, is that of standing both to employ such powers and to resist attempts to restrict this employment in ways that do not place similar limitations on all – a view Guyer's examination of property echoes and reinforces. So understood, the citizen's equality is not merely, or most centrally, testimony to the fact that she is *owed* benefit, and protection from burden, proportionate to what others receive. It flags her status as one with both the authority to assert claims of right or political power and the duty to respect a like authority in fellow citizens.

The reading of political independence that parallels these accounts of civic obligation and standing offers a characterization of lawmaking capacity. More particularly, it addresses capacities to develop, propose and assess standards to regulate both one's own conduct and that of other community members. As I consider more fully in what follows, citizens must see themselves and fellow legislators as in the business of advancing positions on laws and policies put forward for community adoption. Indeed, they must view themselves as proposing such laws and policies after personal evaluation and with the conviction that they will serve justice. To conceive of oneself as a Kantian citizen is also to understand oneself as a participant in developing, proposing and evaluating the standards that will shape every member's actions within a shared political community. This participatory and community-oriented picture, of course, is one to which Williams's reading of the supreme proprietor lends further support.

4.2.1.2   Passive Citizens

Idealization Concerns

Critics and sympathizers alike are bound to wonder, though, whether this participatory account (like minimalism and some middle-ground views) in fact is problematically idealized. After all, it seems to ask us to understand citizens as possessed of developed capacities that many lack and as impervious to the very real barriers many face in exercising these. If so, substantial supports for realized civic participation (a central focus of state-sponsored social welfare on the robust view I have in mind) could not be among the appropriate concerns of the just Kantian state on the civic respect account. For idealized citizens, after all, such supports would be superfluous.

Kant's own remarks regarding "passive citizens" (MM 6: 314–315) seem to confirm this as a concern with deep textual roots. Apparently disqualifying some for full citizenship in light of the negative effects of poverty on realized civic capacities, and blithely leaving the propertyless to fend for themselves in attempts to gain civic membership, such remarks appear good textual evidence for idealization. But this problem is only apparent. Indeed, reasonably interpreted from the perspective of civic respect, Kant's discussion not only avoids the kind of idealization that minimalism in particular embraces. It also suggests that a system of just laws must be sensitive to context, a feature especially important where social welfare supports are at issue.

To appreciate the grounds for defending Kantian justice as both non-idealized and context-sensitive, first return to a standard reading of the paragraphs distinguishing active from passive citizenship.[22] On this interpretation, recall, the active citizen simply corresponds to the ideal with which Kant opens his citizenship discussion. Most importantly, such a citizen is independent, or *sui juris*. In full command of her fate, she makes and acts on her own decisions

---

[22] My discussion of passive citizenship here draws on Holtman (2018).

about how to employ legal rights and powers rather than relying on others to use these on her behalf. As a consequence, she also possesses "civil personality." She represents herself in civic matters that range from voting and enforcing contracts to answering criminal charges (MM 6: 314).

The related understanding of passive citizenship on this standard view draws not only on the *Rechtslehre* passage but also on Kant's similar remarks in "Theory and Practice." Those who do not own and control the resources necessary to support themselves, these together suggest, lack central civic qualifications. Neither independent nor possessed of civil personality, they are underlings who require others' direction and protection (MM 6: 315). True, the *Rechtslehre* discussion makes clear that the state may not deprive such an "associate" or "passive part" of the opportunity to achieve full civic status. But this achievement will come through her own efforts and not via state assistance. Laws and institutions need ensure only that "anyone can *work his way up* from the passive condition to an active one" (MM 6: 315, emphasis added).

So understood, these passages enunciate a kind of test or bar indicating who is included in the class of citizens and who is not. While status is not rigid (except perhaps for women), Kant's seeming commitment to mere formal equality of opportunity means that the passive citizen must look to her own efforts and her good fortune, or perhaps to the charity of others, for a chance to leave the status of underling behind. As standardly understood, then, both in concept and as instantiated in the world, the Kantian citizen must realize certain qualifications. Some who have yet to do so may have the prospect of becoming citizens. But the status is reserved, and the laws designed, for those currently satisfying the criteria. Provided there is formal equality of opportunity, moreover, any change in civic status will depend on an individual's own efforts or good fortune and not on state supports.

But now consider another possibility, one ultimately grounded in civic respect but initially prompted by obvious parallels between Kant's citizen ideal and his *Groundwork* characterization of moral legislators for a kingdom of ends. Unlike the standard view, this more progressive or evolutionary interpretation focuses on basic understandings of moral concepts and methods to which Kant appeals in these separate works.[23] On this view, accounts of moral and political citizenship do not offer qualifications for membership. They rather provide a characterization of, and a model for, active moral and political

---

[23] In appealing to the *Groundwork*, I do not mean to suggest that Kant derives his account of justice from the moral theory or that there are not important differences between the two. I simply offer grounds for seeing his moral and political theories as richly related. Fuller exploration of the nature of this relationship must await another occasion.

participation, as well as a call to facilitate and maintain participation so understood.

It is in keeping with this alternative picture (thus supportive of it) that Kant in fact pursues two different, though mutually supporting, paths in the *Rechtslehre* as he lays the foundations for his accounts of justice and citizenship. The first of these paths (MM 6: 230–231) employs a conceptual analysis of justice similar in style to the conceptual analysis of morality with which he begins the second chapter of the *Groundwork*. The second is the fourfold analysis of freedom as "the only original right belonging to every man by virtue of his humanity" (MM 6: 237). Now familiarly, this innate right of freedom includes not only the classic freedom from force and fraud but also equality of benefit and burden; recognition of each as *sui juris*; and the assumption that each is "beyond reproach," or just, provided she has done nothing implicating another's rights (MM 6: 237–238).

In content, this latter discussion looks back to the kingdom-of-ends characterization of rational agents as free, equal and autonomous; it also looks forward to that of citizens. Importantly, it offers enrichment to the account of justice and its first principle developed through earlier conceptual analysis. Critical for our purposes, it suggests that Kant constructs his conceptions of justice and citizenship, in part, by reference back to foundational elements of his moral theory. Thus we can think of him as asking what free, equal and autonomous legislators would need to attend to in enacting laws duly considerate of the self-governing status of each under circumstances in which issues of security, assurance and under-determination arise. (As we have seen, these are issues that Ripstein's interpretation emphasizes and that others readily acknowledge.) In particular, Kant seems to suggest on this reading, legislators would need to attend: 1) to the allocation of burden and benefit among persons possessed of dignity or incomparable worth; 2) to the possibility that some autonomous agents might come under the direction of others; 3) to the concern that attributions of guilt to these agents could never precede warranted judgments and never be based on anything other than the act in question; and finally 4) to protecting such agents from the effects of force and fraud on freedom of choice and action.

So understood, innate right and related discussions bear importantly on our understanding of the distinction between passive and active citizenship and the accompanying limits on permissible legislation. In particular, they counsel us to read relevant passages as the product of reflecting on how the state must address its members given the barriers to full civic participation that worldly non-idealities (e.g., poverty and gender bias) present. Read in this light, passive citizenship discussions are an invitation to address what Kant sees, given social realities, as serious problems of justice. They suggest what is required if we are to treat fellow citizens with due respect when conditions prevent full realization of civic features. Rather than circumscribing civic membership, the passages on passive citizenship both describe a subset of citizens who require special attention and offer broad, context-sensitive standards for properly addressing those whose present circumstances warrant our concern and action.

In keeping with Kant's texts thoughtfully reread, then, what relevant passages present (and the civic respect reading embraces) is not a membership test. It is an ideal of justice at which to aim and in light of which we must shape our laws, policies and institutions.[24] Although Wood ultimately is more skeptical than I am about Kant's willingness to advocate state-sponsored social welfare, it is worth noting that the passages he emphasizes regarding general injustice support the conclusion that Kant indeed recognized issues plaguing so-called passive citizens as problems of justice. These passages further support the conclusion that, for Kant, such issues demand attention not only to individual actions or particular laws but also to legal systems and institutions as a set. As Kant recognized, these work not only singly but also together to shape relationships and actions within political society.

Implications for Equality of Opportunity

This understanding of the passive/active distinction has further implications for our interpretation of equality of opportunity on Kant's account. Note first that the language of the *Rechtslehre* passage itself is at least ambiguous on this point. Positive laws that comport with justice must not be contrary to citizens' freedom and equality, and thus they must be consistent with the principle that anyone can work up from a passive to an active condition. But if we accept that the legal system is ours to design and to change and that problems of general injustice are ones we have a responsibility to remedy (both conclusions Kant's texts support), then laws cementing deep differences of wealth in place will be among those through which we deny opportunity for full citizenship to a certain social class, religious group or the like. If we further accept that our approach to citizenship issues must be sensitive to the context at hand, again in keeping with Kant's texts, we likewise should reject mere formal equality of opportunity as a standard for determining what supports are adequate to allow passive citizens to develop and exercise civic capacities. Such supports (which might include income redistribution, access to basic education, housing and the like) may be

---

[24] For a reading that understands the passive citizenship discussion very differently, see Pascoe (2015). By contrast, Varden (2006) offers an interpretation that (like mine) posits substantial state responsibilities to "passive" citizens on a Kantian model.

necessary in order to put those in need in a position to do the very real *work* that is developing and exercising the capacities required of citizens.

Of course, further familiar passages in "Theory and Practice" will seem to weigh against this reading, especially those that permit children to inherit family wealth despite exacerbating effects on economic disparities. It is worth considering more carefully, though, in what context Kant makes these remarks and how rigid he likely intends the principle regarding inheritance to be. Especially noteworthy is the fact that here Kant is explaining in what sense citizens of the just state are to be understood as free, equal and independent, most immediately the second. What is most fundamentally at issue when we consider whether the equality of citizens is respected, he is at pains to explain, is not "the quantity and degree of their possessions" (TP 8: 291). It is their equality, as subjects, to coerce each other only "through public law" (TP 8: 292).

Kant's question in this section of "Theory and Practice," then, is not whether laws permitting wealth to pass to children through inheritance could ever be unjust. Likewise, it is not whether another set of laws might be required to secure foundations allowing each to have a genuine opportunity to attain active citizenship. His aim is simply to distinguish the concept of civic equality from equality of property broadly conceived. This supports the conclusion, contra both minimalist and many middle-ground views, that there is no reason to see Kant as here foreclosing the possibility of state-sponsored social welfare supports that provide a foundation for active citizenship. It also confirms that an account of equality of opportunity more robust than a merely formal one is reasonably understood as both in the spirit of Kant's political theory and in the letter.

4.2.1.3   The General Will

Likewise central in understanding the nature and role of Kantian citizens on a civic respect reading is a rendering of the general will. Again, this "general united will of the people" is the legislative will. The requirement that it ground state laws ensures that we properly understand each citizen to make arrangements for herself and thus to suffer no injustice when coerced to comply (MM 6: 313–314).

As already noted, there is wide agreement that, for Kant, the general will that connects laws with citizen decision-making is not what a majority endorses, but, as Rosen puts it, what "an entire people could rationally consent to" (Rosen, 1993, p. 23). The civic respect account, however, rejects the further view (one minimalists and middle-ground theorists like Rosen share) that this is consent given, most fundamentally, from a self-focused or individualist perspective. Rather, civic respect equates general and rational consent with what citizens unanimously would choose as laws to govern the state as a whole from the perspective of free, equal, independent and responsible members who are at once makers of law and subject to it. These are members committed to each not only as individual citizens possessed of, or in the process of developing or revising, a conception of the good, but also (and as centrally) as participating parties in the shared project that is the just state.

Favoring this reading from the perspective of citizenship and joint endeavor is, first, the fact that Kant introduces the *Rechtslehre* characterization of citizenship by appeal to the general or legislative will. This suggests the two conceptions are tightly linked. Further recommending it is the foregoing understanding of passive citizenship not as a rule of exclusion, but as an acknowledgment of obstacles to participatory membership and a demand for legislative supports toward realized independence. The just system that citizens endorse from the perspective of the general will is one actively committed to the civic development of each. Especially in the context of laws governing the acquisition and distribution of property, moreover, Williams's analysis of Kant's supreme proprietor not only harmonizes with but also strengthens this reading. No matter what physical person or group fulfills the function in a given political society, we must understand the determinations of the supreme proprietor properly to regulate property broadly conceived so as equally and adequately to support the functioning of each society member as individual citizen and agent. In this the supreme proprietor exemplifies the appropriate deliverances of the general will, what each would choose to serve every citizen so conceived.[25]

4.2.1.4 Summing Up

From this rereading of *Rechtslehre* passages on the citizen ideal and the general will, we should take the following. First, what is central not only to seeing oneself as a Kantian citizen, but to addressing or respecting others as such, is a realized appreciation for each member's status as an authorized adopter and rejecter, as well as a proposer and evaluator, of civil laws, policies and institutions. It is further to see oneself as at once a claimholder under the laws and as charged with the duty to respect others' rightful claims. Second, as the characterization that gives content to the freedom that justice protects, this account of citizenship also describes the general scope and content of justice as Kant understands it. Justice requires citizens and the laws and institutions to which

---

[25] The helpful discussion of political judgment in Kaufman (1999), ch. 5, further supports this picture of the general will and civic perspective.

they commit themselves actively to respect the freedom of each so conceived. Hence the description of this interpretation as a civic respect account. Third, to demonstrate this kind of respect for one another, lawmaking citizens, and the standards they adopt, must attend not only to the general elements that together compose the citizen ideal, but also to the ways in which worldly conditions affect individuals' ability successfully to exercise citizenship so understood. This means that the laws, policies and institutions that ultimately embody justice not only may vary with place and time but also must do so. Together with other elements of the citizen perspective, this variation is part of what is necessary for standards to be ones to which each can be deemed to give her rational consent, part of what is required for legal standards properly to be described as backed by the general will. Again, such variation is also crucial if justice (via the laws that give it voice) is successfully to address questions of social welfare.

4.2.2 Private Right

Of course both minimalist and many middle-ground theories draw significantly on Kant's discussion of private right to interpret his account of justice and assess the place of state-sponsored social welfare within it. Any adequate response from those rejecting the force and fraud model, then, must engage this topic. Supplementing my own discussion with Guyer's like-minded views, this section considers private right from the perspective of civic respect. In keeping with our limited purposes, the focus is on Kant's basic account of property claims and acquisitions.

As we have seen, minimalists understand the discussion of private right in the *Rechtslehre*'s first central section at least to flag property and contractual rights as ones at the core of justice as Kant understands it. Some hold that we can acquire such rights without the state and in advance of its establishment, thus creating claims that it is bound to honor. Although they do not accept this view, middle-ground theorists like Rosen and Ripstein agree that, in addition to bodily integrity, rights of property and contract are those with which the Kantian state is most concerned. In a particularly detailed treatment, Ripstein characterizes Kant's account of private right as one that sets forth the funda-mental categories of justice-relevant relationships in the realm of acquired right. Although he acknowledges some difficulties regarding domestic right, property and contract strike Ripstein as unproblematically related to an under-lying picture of persons (and citizens) as purposive agents concerned to develop and pursue ends and plans. Each type of ownership claim thus comes in for special protection in the Kantian state as Ripstein envisions it.

There is no doubt that Kant thinks of property and contract as areas likely to raise issues of justice. That is, they are likely (most broadly viewed) to bring the choices and actions of one person into conflict with those of another in ways inconsistent with foundational principles. But a closer look at the way Kant conducts the discussion of private right and positions it within his larger argument supports the conclusion that it is a mistake to read him as any of the aforementioned minimalist and middle-ground theorists do.

This discussion in fact proceeds as we should expect it to given the basic aims and structure of the *Rechtslehre* itself. As is clear from his conceptual analysis of justice in the *Rechtslehre* introduction, and from his characterizations of freedom and citizenship, Kant is not concerned here to identify the content of justice in any concrete way. His aim is more plausibly to consider the relationships that make justice necessary. Given his general characterization of justice, these will be relationships that bring the chosen actions of one person into conflict with those of others. In light of the analysis just presented, they also will be relationships that implicate our ability to acknowledge one another as free, equal, independent and responsible citizens. On Kant's view, as we have seen, this is possible only through a state that effectively acknowledges these citizen features via shared laws and institutions that demonstrate civic respect. Among the relationships the legal system must address in this way will be those that come under the private right heading. Relationships of private right thus are ones the just state and its citizens will define, interpret and police, not ones that will themselves govern state and citizens as it were from on high.

When Kant specially addresses the right to a thing as involving a relationship among persons, then, we best understand him to invoke the ideas presented earlier with the particular aim of dispelling the sometimes popular notion that property rights mark some special connection between a person and an object that others must honor. When he speaks of a right to a thing as assuming "possession in common with all others" (MM 6: 276), or claims that we must understand all nations to "stand originally in a community of land" and a "community of possible physical interaction" (MM 6: 352), we should likewise interpret him with an eye to the conditions in which questions of justice arise. We must see ourselves as sharing a community with one another with respect to movables, land and the like because any use that we make of these as individuals potentially impacts the choices and actions of others, in particular the similar uses they might make. In the absence of an independent connection between persons and objects that merits recognition, we must regulate these matters impacting choice and action, like others, via a standard to which all could consent as free, equal, independent and responsible persons. Such a standard must be one that the community of interest sanctions through laws all can share because they are laws duly respectful of each. As Guyer emphasizes, this community-oriented perspective on the material and other matters that are candidates for ownership is especially appropriate because of their central role in sustaining life and in supporting the successful setting and pursuit of our ends. Understood from the perspective of civic respect, these last include not only ends we hold as individuals but also those central to our civic participation both domestic and global.

More certainly could be said. But putting Kant's discussion in context is sufficient to show that he intends his treatment of private right to place relations among individuals with regard to matters in which we are accustomed to claim personal ownership on a par with other issues of justice. So far from acknowledging categories of relationship to which states must give special treatment, Kant here denies that property, contract and domestic relations are different in kind from other associations or connections that may implicate justice. These are relationships that we create and that we are duty-bound to shape in ways that are respectful of each as a citizen.

We may, of course, be sorely tempted to see property relationships differently. Nevertheless, only their centrality to our existence and possibilities distinguishes them from other associations or interactions in which the choice of one may affect those of others in ways that implicate the kind of participatory citizenship among end-setting agents described earlier. And this difference only makes our active role in shaping property-related laws with an eye to civic respect the more crucial.

4.2.3 Justice and Poverty Relief

This overview of the civic respect account puts us in a position to engage state-sponsored social welfare more directly from a new interpretive vantage. In this section, I begin in the obvious place, with the *Rechtslehre* discussion of domestic poverty relief to which we have returned several times. While I note and defend general departures from both minimalist and middle-ground interpretations throughout, Subsection 4.2.3.2 gives specific attention to disagreements with Ripstein and O'Neill. All of this paves the way for the promised illustrative applications in Sections 4.2.4 and 4.2.5.

4.2.3.1 The *Rechtslehre* Passage in Review

Among the rights "that follow from the nature of the civil union," says Kant, as we know, is the state's right to tax the citizenry for the support of those "unable to provide for even their most necessary natural needs" (MM 6: 326). Whatever its deeper foundations, he indicates that this right to tax derives from the people's duty and stems from a more general right of the state "to impose taxes on the people for its own preservation" (MM 6: 325–326). Support for the poor is one of the potential uses for these preservation-related tax monies (MM 6: 326). To further establish that a state may tax to relieve poverty in particular, Kant reminds readers that the "general will" of the people unites us in an ongoing society and submits to the state's authority to insure perpetual maintenance. Elaborating, he adds that we submit to such authority to "maintain those members of the society who are unable to maintain themselves" (MM 6: 326).

Perhaps Kant has in mind, as minimalists suggest, that no society can maintain itself without insuring basic sustenance for some number of citizens. This, again, would be required not merely so that the state would have a populace but also to make various cooperative efforts possible, to perform government functions and to produce future generations. Beyond criticisms Rosen and others offer, though, this minimalist interpretation is a poor rendering of the passage's language. First, Kant does not refer to stability directly. He straightforwardly equates society's maintenance with the sustenance of individual members. Second, his justification for imposing tax burdens on the rich is neither that it is necessary for the protection and care of the wealthy nor that it is warranted by the needs of the state. Taxes are justified because they will be used to satisfy the needs of the people. Though these needs would certainly include social stability, they would not be limited to it. Finally, and in keeping with Guyer and Williams's observations, reference to the general will – in which each participates *qua* citizen – recalls the larger account of justice and its demand that we respect each as a free, equal, independent and responsible member of society. This further invokes the individual as the focus of concern.

From this emphasis on the individual we might suppose, with Rosen, that the state's right to tax for poverty relief derives instead from the duty of benevolence or charity, a duty that binds all individual members as rational agents. But this reading is unwarranted. Notice, in particular, that Kant embeds the passage in a detailed discussion of the nature and justification of the state. Thus if we want to know from what duty the state's right stems, we should surely appeal to the reason for which (according to Kant) we unite in an ongoing society. And this, we have now seen, is the concern to ensure respect for the multifaceted and politically engaged freedom of each that is at the heart of Kantian justice.[26] It is

---

[26] One might think Kant's reference to the state's "right" to impose taxes rather than its "duty" supports Rosen's view. But Kant speaks in terms of rights throughout this discussion of the state. This includes the discussion of punishment, though on his view justice requires state punishment for every proven criminal. More, while duties of virtue possess a flexibility those of justice do not, whether we fulfill them is not up to us; they indeed are duties. The language of "right,"

also worth noting that the passage supplies no reason to suppose that any justice-based relief it envisions is limited to efforts to protect the poor from force and fraud, as middle-ground and minimalist theorists all would have it.

Of further relevance in assessing the benevolence-based view, Kant also tells us that the duty the state assumes here is one that authorizes coercive taxes on the wealthy to provide the poor with the very means of sustenance, to address "their most necessary natural needs" (MM 6: 326). The concern, then, is not with the barriers to happiness in general that might speak for an underlying duty of benevolence. It is with basic needs. Kant also expands further here on the reason for which we form the state, noting that the wealthy (but presumably others as well) submit to the state's authority (or rightly can be taken to do so) because they require its "protection and care . . . in order to live" (MM 6: 326).

For Kant it thus seems, whether wealthy or poor we form the state and rely on its laws and institutions to maintain ourselves as agents who are free in the complex sense surveyed earlier in this Element. The state (best seen as ourselves in our role as citizens) fulfills this shared purpose, at least in part, by securing the basic needs of each. For some, this will mean protecting morally legitimate property holdings. For others, it will mean providing state-funded material, educational or other supports. What precisely these will be and how best these supports are made available will vary with place, time and circumstances. But providing for needs foundational to agency is fundamental to the very purpose of the state, thus not something it (or we) can choose to forgo. More, whether the state attends to such needs through laws protecting property or laws providing material and other supports, not only the grounds of decision, but also the energy and material, are part of our shared effort. The project that is the just state is a joint or community endeavor, in part, because both the reasons that ground state laws and the assets the state makes possible are ones in which each citizen shares and whose essentially mutual character each properly acknowledges.

4.2.3.2   Regarding Mendicancy and Reach

For all that we have said so far, though, it might still be true that the relief Kant sanctions is limited, as Ripstein claims, to ensuring that no one is relegated to the position of mendicant. Nor does our discussion thus far address O'Neill's worry that a justice whose reach extends beyond force and fraud would

---

then, provides no reason to suppose that state-funded poverty relief concerns what the state may do and not what it must. At most it seems to suggest that the state might address poverty by more than one route, compulsory taxation being not only acceptable, but for Kant preferred.

fruitlessly acknowledge rights claims we could not hope to satisfy, ultimately weakening our ability to address agency-threatening need.

As we have seen, Kant himself recognizes poverty as a particular threat to citizenship because of the way it undercuts the ability to choose and act for oneself in public matters. One who depends on another for basic needs, lacking control over the implements of her trade and even a developed talent that might render her self-sufficient, becomes a tool for others' use. We should also presume, he suggests, that she is a second vote of support for whatever representative, law or policy the person offering to fulfill such needs might favor. This indeed seems to be the principal textual ground for Ripstein's conclusion.

On the richer civic respect reading, though, support that saves one from the life of a beggar is only the beginning of what justice requires where poverty is at issue. To respect a person's civic capacities as justice demands is to take her seriously not merely as a person who ought not be relegated to the position of slave or mouthpiece of another. She must also be able to function meaningfully as a developer and evaluator of laws and the like, and she must be reasonably positioned to act in accord with those laws in constructing and pursuing a life plan. As important, she must be positioned to appreciate others as fellow participants in political life and in the contributions citizens together make to the more personal life of each individual.

Poverty threatens such civic capacities in many ways. It undermines self-respect, breeds contempt between economic classes, cripples mutual appreciation through lack of shared experience and much more. Even if the Kantian state attempts to offer goods like education, health care and accessible public spaces to all on equal terms, poverty can subvert that equality. It can render these goods inaccessible in part due to the ills of diminished self-respect and class animosity, but also due to the interaction of these goods with differences in opportunity and experience that familiarly go hand in hand with differences in wealth.

One may argue, of course, that Kant did not see this, or that he saw it and nevertheless determined that protections for private property or a tough-minded insistence on pulling oneself up by one's own bootstraps was more consistent with justice. But given justifications we now have for understanding Kant's views on citizenship, property and opportunity so differently from the interpretations minimalists and middle-ground theorists offer, there is good reason to discount these arguments. More, though Kant himself neither expressly advocates more extensive measures to address wealth inequality nor develops a full-blown conception of fair equality of opportunity, we have found good grounds to think that each fits his foundational views better than the alternative. An account including each, then, would be Kantian in spirit (as Wood in fact suggests).

As we expand the conception of Kantian justice, though, what is the cost? Do we have the material means, ingenuity and energy meaningfully to acknowledge such claims? Do we do better, with O'Neill, to leave justice as long tradition saw it, with the prevention of force and fraud – or of coercion and deception? Should we recognize as claims of right those fundamentally rooted in prohibitions that we have a reasonable chance of addressing and let obligations of virtue, sometimes assumed and facilitated by state institutions, do the rest?

Here I think the answer is to consider what it would be satisfactorily to address a question of justice on the Kantian view I have described. The worry that the claims of right that justice cognizes may be impossible to satisfy if they move from the realm of negative prohibition to that of positive action misses the import of Kant's view, at least as I understand it. This is first because justice, for Kant, is in part aspirational. While some states come closer to realizing justice than others, the citizen ideal (and the laws and institutions that might make it a reality) are ones we nowhere fully realize. Together with the republican ideal of *Perpetual Peace*, these offer a goal or limit at which to aim. Moreover, in keeping with Kant's own recognition of a context-sensitive justice (one O'Neill herself applauds), there is no blueprint here for states to follow. Even those that most closely approach the ideal surely will need to alter and sometimes abandon previously successful measures as conditions change over time.[27]

Second, what Kant's account of justice as civic respect requires is not that we fulfill any specific set of claims. It is rather that we develop laws, institutions and policies from the appropriate perspective, and then evaluate and revisit them as new information comes in. This is not to say that we thus do justice simply by doing our best. Indeed, we should often expect to find, on reevaluation, that we erred in some way we could or should have avoided, doing injustice then and after as we implemented our mistake (or perhaps as often, our culpable self-dealing or prejudice). It is to say, though, that the most fundamental requirement of Kantian justice demands that we make and act on laws from the perspective of civic respect sketched earlier in this Element. Given this, there is reason to think that O'Neill's worries about energy and resources may be less significant than she imagines.

---

[27] For somewhat different though complementary reasons, both this and the remaining points regarding O'Neill are ones Williams too embraces.

Finally, and relatedly, justice on the civic respect view I have described takes account of the resources we have, the ill aims and institutional errors with which we must deal and much more. What it asks of us is not that we do precisely this or that. It is that we design a set of laws and the like that take persons seriously as citizens under the circumstances in which we now find ourselves while seeking to work toward domestic and cosmopolitan ideals over time. It is a position that neither demands that we do more than is possible at this moment nor allows us to rest content morally speaking.

In light of this, expanding justice beyond the realm of coercion and deception, even as O'Neill broadly conceives them, seems not only textually but practically warranted. The approach I have sketched does not demand the impossible of us now. It does acknowledge the profound moral import of matters (poverty among them) that threaten the realization of citizenship and individual agency as I have understood them. It also demands that we employ our ingenuity and our energy, that we strive to maintain what some have called Kantian patriotism (Kleingeld, 2000), and that we work toward the wider aim of a genuinely cosmopolitan outlook. These matters are not merely motivating, lighting a fire under us or calling attention to real privations we might otherwise ignore or overlook. They are guides, helping us to determine what to consider, work on and investigate, and what lens or glass to use as we do. For creatures such as we, this aspect of Kantian justice is crucial, and one we cannot afford to set aside even for the valuable companion lens that is Kantian virtue.

4.2.4 Domestic Support

On Kant's view as I understand it, then, the way in which to address issues of state-sponsored social welfare like that of domestic poverty depends very much on the conditions at hand and the work of citizens and representatives on the joint project that is their state. This does not mean that a concrete illustration is counter to the spirit of Kant's views. Indeed, Kant himself frequently appeals to this kind of explanatory and guiding aid, and in this section and the next I do the same. While conclusions are always open to debate and circumstances in any particular case may vary in relevant ways, the reasons and considerations on offer can both clarify the civic respect approach and provide insights to inform debates on the ground. To this end, here I extend the theoretic discussion by considering several questions relevant to the just development or reform of a system of state poverty relief. Expanding the discussion to cosmopolitan contexts, Section 4.2.5 takes up foreign aid to child victims of disaster. As noted earlier, each example focuses on the perspective or attitude that we properly adopt in addressing matters of justice on the civic respect model and on what would be relevant in developing standards duly considerate of the citizenship and personhood of each from that point of view.[28]

Rather than attempting to capture in a single example the kind of variation that circumstances inevitably will demand, in discussing domestic relief in this section, I assume a state of relative wealth and circumstances where emergencies like war or epidemic do not currently demand the bulk of lawmakers' attention or of society's resources. The questions I treat are ones commonly raised in contemporary, Western democracies. They are whether state relief: 1) unfairly burdens those required to fund it and unfairly benefits recipients; 2) renders recipients dependent or childlike; or 3) undermines personal virtues of responsibility or self-sufficiency. Any of these implications or tendencies, of course, is one legislators would view with concern from the perspective of Kantian civic respect. As we consider what it would be take up this perspective with these problems in view, the aim again is to clarify the approach itself and to gain a clearer sense of its practical implications and the foundations underlying them.[29]

4.2.4.1 Special Treatment

In affluent Western democracies, critics often allege that state-sponsored programs designed to relieve poverty unfairly burden the better off. Indeed, even those who favor welfare provisions often agree that the poor take something extra from the state that the wealthy do not. On the Kantian civic respect view I have sketched, by contrast, those needing monetary assistance do not differ from those requiring protection for their property. From this perspective, we properly see all as vulnerable when it comes to physical and psychological essentials. Some need the state to defend the extant holdings that support their civic and personal development and action; others require it for assistance in attaining the material and other goods necessary for life and agency both civic and personal. Neither case indicates, without more, that need or willingness to accept aid has its source in any moral failing or that assistance best is seen as largesse. Rather, on Kant's view so understood, a central aim of the joint endeavor that is the just state is assuring each member equal access to what sustains life and founds civic and personal

---

[28] Again, what kinds of welfare supports best will address threats to agency in the historical, cultural and other circumstances at hand; how we balance these with other justice-related concerns where resources are scarce; how we structure, publicize and promote social welfare supports so that both direct beneficiaries and those whose needs lie elsewhere can endorse them as required elements of their joint project – all are issues legislators for particular states must address for relevant contexts. Answers thus necessarily will vary from state to state and over time.

[29] Examples draw on Holtman (2004).

development. Poverty relief (which itself may take many forms) is one route among many to fulfilling this commitment.

4.2.4.2   Dependency

Both advocates and opponents also appeal to troubling connections between state-sponsored poverty relief and the independence of those who receive it. Public assistance must thwart this quality, they worry, since a person who believes she can count on the state to support her loses a taste for self-reliance and becomes a lazy, childlike ward.

Kantian civic respect, by contrast, understands the concerns at the forefront of such debates as most likely to materialize where we forgo public support, leaving the poor to seek assistance from the better off and to become as a consequence their wards or servants. When we are dependent on others to supply our most basic needs, Kant's discussion of passive citizenship observes, it is difficult for us to see ourselves, and at least equally for others to see us, as capable of competently evaluating options on our own or acting on the resulting judgments. But viewed from the perspective of civic respect, the assistance of the just Kantian state differs in kind from that of the private philanthropist. For state laws, policies and institutions on this model adopt and pursue our own commitments to ensuring respect for the freedom, equality, independence and responsibility of each.

Importantly, this outlook thus supports strong Kant-based criticism of some recently popular approaches to relief in the affluent states under discussion. Consider, for instance, periodic advocacy (especially in the United States) for instituting strict employment requirements applicable to adult welfare recipients. With critics of these requirements, Kant would share worries that so-called welfare-to-work schemes may abandon those in need to jobs that fail to pay a living wage and to consequent privations in the realm of basic needs. The perspective of civic respect, though, carries criticism of such proposals beyond these significant concerns of sustenance. It warns us, first, to be alert to the messages we send through our chosen brand of poverty relief. If a welfare system imposes, e.g., lifetime limits insensitive to circumstance and severe penalties for those who fail to follow job-seeking rules to the letter, its message is that we are each on our own in securing survival basics and that those who do not toe the line will suffer the consequences. This advocates no joint commitment to the development of each as citizen and individual, but rather the callous isolation that comes with commitment to one's own interest above all.

The perspective of civic respect further reminds us to examine more tangible impacts on independence and other citizen characteristics by attending, for example, to the nature of the jobs that would replace relief payments. Do these encourage or thwart the development of a critical outlook? Do they leave time for workers to develop or maintain relationships with friends, spouses and children or otherwise to progress as members of a political body or as individuals? Are prevalent working conditions those we associate with independence or with subjugation? Suppose that too many of the available jobs exhaust bodies and numb minds, that scant pay and benefits mean little free time, that management engages in demeaning or threatening practices. Under such circumstances, we may conclude that these jobs stifle the ability to evaluate laws and policies, to develop a plan of life or to foster the mutual concern and respect that are part of Kantian citizenship fully realized.

None of this suggests that concerns about the relationship between state-funded relief and dependency are not ones Kantians must share. To the extent a system fosters such dependence, reform is in order. From the viewpoint of civic respect, though, the independence justice requires us to seek is a rich notion importantly distinct from the ability to pursue one's own interest and extending well beyond the ability to secure shelter and sustenance or even freedom from coercion and deception. It is an independence that includes not only personal and political development but also an appreciation of one's place in a community of individuals committed to one another.

4.2.4.3   Social Virtue

Finally, a Kantian approach to state-sponsored relief, framed by views on justice and citizenship as understood on the civic respect account, can respond to popular calls to hard work, to self-reliance and to personal responsibility in the form of thrift. Certainly, Kantians may acknowledge these three traits as virtues with moral consequence. They may help us appropriately to value our own talents and capabilities and to show others respect by not unduly imposing on their limited energies and means. But the relationship of these virtues to the ends of a state-sponsored social welfare system does not make them criteria by which to judge or redesign it.

A system of state-sponsored relief perhaps should seek to support virtues. For on Kant's view, these are settled commitments that aid us in fulfilling moral demands, including those of justice. If we shape the welfare system in part to foster virtue, though, it should be virtue that rests on the concerns of justice that are the system's proper focus. To further Kantian justice on the civic respect model, we must aim to encourage the better off to recognize that they are as beholden to the state as those who require its financial assistance, that each likewise is equally deserving of that assistance and that each is an equal member of a political community founded on these mutual obligations and claims. We further must aim for a system that encourages the financially needy to understand support not as a handout from others, but as a share of joint assets set aside to be used whenever a member of the group faces a genuine threat to fundamentals. As such we must see it as one form of self-support (thus an affirmation of self-respect, not a threat to it) and as one's responsibility to maintain (thus not to be depleted unduly or unnecessarily). Given this, there is a virtue that a welfare system on the civic respect model should seek to foster, and that would help to ensure its proper functioning. Unlike any of those so often named (each of which is separate from justice), it is the internalization of our commitment to justice itself. We might call it the virtue of civic respect.

4.2.5 State-Sponsored Social Welfare in Cosmopolitan Contexts

In Kant's own time, war and colonialism took pride of place among issues of cosmopolitan justice (ones involving interactions among foreign states and citizens). In ours, obligations of social welfare have joined them, and no Kant-based discussion of state-sponsored social welfare could be complete without some consideration of the cosmopolitan implications of Kantian theory in this regard. Even more than in the domestic setting, though, such questions are both many and varied and highly sensitive to context. So here I illustrate the cross-border implications of Kantian civic respect for a circumscribed case. The aim is to suggest some of the considerations most central to such discussions from this standpoint, as well as the direction and perspective it urges us to adopt. Because the civic respect reading is in harmony with Williams's views regarding obligations to provide foreign aid, the focus in this final substantive section is instead on considerations that should shape the nature of what we offer and the methods we employ.

The general example I consider is that of relief to foreign children suffering threats to basic needs in the wake of a disaster not of the benefactor state's making (war, famine, epidemic or similar catastrophe).[30] I choose it because, assuming the beneficiary's home state remains intact, it offers a clear case in which that state's justice-relevant obligations, institutions and practices, as well as those of home-state citizens, require due consideration. It is worth noting, to set the stage, that while Kant does not treat such cases in detail, his discussion of private right acknowledges parental obligations of justice toward developing children. In the *Rechtslehre*, he also identifies children as passive citizens with the potential to work their way to active status, thus as the focus of further obligations of justice (these borne by the home state and fellow citizens). Taken

---

[30] The discussion here has its basis in Holtman (2006).

together with his treatment of poverty relief, then, the assumption of domestic obligations of justice to children in need within a Kantian framework is more than reasonable. As we see in what follows, appropriately acknowledging such domestic obligations and the relationships that ground them is central to demonstrating Kantian civic respect in a cosmopolitan setting. It must shape our approach to state-sponsored social welfare aimed at foreign states and citizens.

4.2.5.1 Competing Contemporary Views

Without offering details, then, we assume both a home state and fellow citizens who are bound to children by domestic obligations of justice regarding basic needs, obligations they cannot currently fulfill. These may fall to parents or to extended family and neighbors in keeping with established practices, as well as to state agencies charged with addressing children as developing citizens.

Against this background, we can better appreciate the outlook on aid that the civic respect approach countenances by contrasting it with two other popular possibilities, ones I term *blithe humanitarianism* and *intervention skepticism*. The first advances its call for aid chiefly as a means of alleviating children's exposure to violence, victimization and disease. Often, such humanitarians further seek to augment children's inadequate developmental opportunities. For these aid proponents, the individual child and her safety and development are the principal focus. From their perspective, considerations relevant to the maintenance and maturation of the individual as community member, likewise the repair and strengthening of justice-based practices and institutions in the home state, are largely side issues.

Operating as a sometimes-stinging counterpoint, international intervention skepticism flags this understanding of child welfare as far too narrow. For the basic needs of any child, proponents urge, include not only the physical, psychological and developmental ones humanitarians emphasize, but also each child's respect for herself as a member of one or more domestic communities (e.g., ethnic, religious or linguistic). It is not enough, says the skeptic, that attention to other basic needs allows the child to develop physical, emotional and intellectual capacities central to functioning in this role. She must learn to see or identify herself as a community member. With its focus on providing for the needs of unfortunate individuals, blithe humanitarianism is more likely to undermine than to foster such an outlook, with dire consequences for children and communities. Moreover, states, individuals and organizations that follow the humanitarian in ignoring this danger, or denying its moral significance, engage in a variety of injustice. They fail to acknowledge and support persons and communities as appropriately self-determining entities.

To the extent they offer aid at all, then, say intervention skeptics, foreign states and citizens should seek not to save individual children, or indeed children *as* individuals. Instead, they should provide what funding they do to foreign communities (local, ethnic, religious or national) for use in strengthening those domestic institutions most likely to foster or sustain these children. Whether even this variety of aid is justifiable, though, is a matter potential providers must always consider. For on this view, foreign aid inevitably is a crutch that threatens to foster home-state dependency and to undermine the very strengths it should support, or to shape laws and institutions in the beneficiary community to conform to the benefactor's vision. On pain of injustice, then, those contemplating aid must carefully evaluate both the form in which to offer it and to whom.

Importantly distinct from these views, but sharing several of their central values and concerns, is the Kant-based civic respect alternative I call *state-centered cosmopolitanism*. On this view, states and citizens addressing issues of cross-border justice (including those now before us) properly view foreign citizens and nations as what we might call "fellow citizens of the world." We must see them, as Kant's third definitive principle for perpetual peace and the accompanying discussion of hospitality suggest, as individuals to whom each of us owes more than the mere moral minimum (e.g., of refraining from unwarranted harming or killing). Further, the state-centered cosmopolitan maintains, states are themselves a species of moral person and bear a special relationship to their own citizens. Grounded both in the features of participatory membership (discussed earlier) and in the prohibition on states' forcible interference in foreign constitutions (found among Kant's preliminary principles for peace), this is a relationship foreign states and citizens must duly respect on pain of injustice.

One of these requirements, of course, pulls in the direction of state-sponsored international aid and the other (at least in certain circumstances) opposes it. What allows the cosmopolitan to hold these potentially conflicting positions without inconsistency, and what most distinguishes her from humanitarians and intervention skeptics, are the Kantian grounds foundational to her view. With Kant, the cosmopolitan agrees that we have moral obligations (both of beneficence and justice) extending to all of our fellow human beings. While these include obligations to address shared basic physical, emotional and psychological needs, from this Kant-based perspective it is moral agency that is essential to any person's humanity and so to treating her with due respect or regard. We must understand persons as moral agents, says the cosmopolitan, in two senses, or, perhaps better, from two perspectives. Viewed individually, each person functions as a moral agent when she employs (or seeks to engage) a capacity to develop and pursue a plan or conception of a valuable life and to commit herself to a set of moral principles to regulate that life. Call this individual agency. Full realization of moral agency, though, also requires participation with others in the joint project of developing, enacting and employing just laws and institutions to regulate life within a smaller subset of humanity. This is civic agency. If we are to treat fellow citizens broadly conceived (and indeed ourselves) as morality and justice demand, we must honor moral agency in both senses.

The state-centered cosmopolitan thus agrees with the humanitarian that, as states and individuals, we have moral obligations to foreigners, among them child victims of disaster. For the cosmopolitan, though, the child as potential citizen, as well as her fellow citizens and her home state, are more complex moral entities than the humanitarian admits. As a consequence of these complexities, justice and morality demand that, in designing aid, we be sensitive to the development of each recipient both as a self-governing person and as a citizen able and disposed to participate in the governance of her local community and her home country. This likewise will require attention to the moral status of the home state and fellow citizens. Such sensitivity applies in particular to parents and others whose relevant moral obligations, institutionally defined and otherwise, are particularly extensive. It must likewise take special account of the home-state laws and institutions that constitute the current political community and whose gradual reform toward a republic of active citizens would be the basis of its progress in the direction of greater justice.

The cosmopolitan thus likewise shares with the intervention skeptic a concern that aid may undermine individual prospects for robust community membership. But she also has a richer conception than the skeptic of community and citizenship, a conception in which we are ideally governors of our own lives, active participants in domestic governance and working members of an international community of persons. As a consequence, she rejects the skeptic's narrow moral analysis of the circumstances justifying or demanding international aid efforts and of the appropriate nature of those efforts themselves.

For the state-centered cosmopolitan, it will be important, for example, to support community practices and related state institutions that understand children as members of families that extend beyond biological parents and siblings to distant relations and even to neighbors. This may require aid aimed at maintaining children within these communities rather than in state or private institutions that ignore or even undermine the practices that cement civic ties, foster a sense of shared membership or play a foundational role in life plans. It may prohibit relief that would remove children from their communities (for example, through adoption) as a means of securing their safety in this time of emergency. But contrary to intervention skepticism, this concern (and aid-related decisions) will not have its foundation in the notion that community practices are valuable in and of themselves. It will arise from recognition that such practices represent one way of joining members in a community of individual and civic agents and of supporting their development as such. And to the extent that practices in fact work to thwart the agency and development of some (perhaps of female children or of those of certain ethnicities), it will withhold or reshape aid with the gradual realization of individual and civic agency and the greater justice of the state as its aim.

4.3 A Brief Overview

Broadly speaking, interpretations of Kant's political philosophy that reject a rigid connection between justice and the prevention of force and fraud seek to integrate the varying elements of Kant's views by appeal to his accounts of personal and political agency. These interpretations differ in the features of Kant's texts that they take to be most telling where state-sponsored social welfare is at issue (e.g., general injustice, private right, the supreme proprietor or the citizen ideal). Yet each offers a reading that significantly enriches the minimalist and middle-ground pictures of civic responsibility on the one hand and of civic development on the other. In so doing, each illuminates connections among the elements of Kant's texts (e.g., the discussions of private property and poverty relief) that are otherwise difficult to appreciate. Each also details a rich and distinctive picture of the Kantian state and citizenry and of the relationships among them. On these views, responsibilities of justice in the realm of social welfare have their source not in the self-focused aims of individuals or even in a more outward-looking concern to prevent deception or unjustified coercion. Instead, such responsibilities are founded in an agency that is both personal and joint and whose successful development and exercise requires the support of each and all.

Concluding Remarks

The interpretive state of affairs on the subject of Kant and state-sponsored social welfare is puzzling at best. How can some read Kant's texts to favor a night watchman state that offers welfare supports only to secure its own survival while others understand the same writings to demand such supports where needed to secure agency richly conceived? That the source of these differences lies in disparate interpretations of the underlying theory of justice provides an explanation, but may only increase the puzzlement. If Kant offers a coherent political theory, why do interpreters read it in so many and conflicting ways?

Part of the answer to this last question surely lies in the difficulty not only of parsing Kant's language and arguments but also of analyzing the relationships among his wide-ranging writings in moral and political philosophy. In my discussion here, I have certainly sought to dispel any notion that Kant's views, whether on justice or on state-sponsored social welfare, are less than coherent. More centrally and importantly, I have provided the kind of careful analysis of competing views that allows us intelligently to choose among them on interpretive grounds and to decide, on moral ones, whether they are worthy of our adoption and extension.

I have argued that the family of Kantian views rejecting a force-and-fraud model is preferable to others on textual grounds. I have also maintained that these views, and the civic respect account in particular, are morally attractive for their broad and context-sensitive understanding of agency, for their appreciation of Kant's commitment to the idea that the state is an importantly joint endeavor and for their ability to speak to a variety of venues, domestic and international. In a world where poverty is commonplace, and where other threats to agency that state-sponsored social welfare might alleviate are far from rare, the Kantian approach, so understood, is one we have good reason to embrace.

Sources

Byrd, B. Sharon and Hruschka, Joachim (2010). *Kant's Doctrine of Right: A Commentary.* Cambridge: Cambridge University Press.

Gregor, Mary (1963). *Laws of Freedom.* New York, NY: Barnes and Noble.

Guyer, Paul (2000). *Kant on Freedom, Law and Happiness.* New York, NY: Cambridge University Press.

Hayek, Friedrich A. (1976). *Law, Legislation and Liberty,* Volume II: *The Mirage of Social Justice.* Chicago, IL: University of Chicago Press.

Holtman, Sarah (2004). "Kantian Justice and Poverty Relief," *Kant-Studien,* 95(1), 86–106.

   (2006). "On the Question of Orphans," *Social Theory and Practice,* 32(4), 579–600.

   (2014). "Kant, Justice and Civic Fellowship," in *Politics and Teleology in Kant (Political Philosophy Now),* ed. Paul Formosa, Avery Goldman and Tatiana Patrone. Cardiff: University of Wales Press, 110–127.

   (2018). "Citizenship and Moral Status," in *Nature and Freedom: Proceedings of the XII International Kant Congress,* ed. Violetta L. Waibel, Margit Ruffing and David Wagner. Berlin: De Gruyter.

Kant, Immanuel (1996). *Practical Philosophy.* Ed. and trans. Mary Gregor. Cambridge: Cambridge University Press.

Kaufman, Alexander (1999). *Welfare in the Kantian State.* Oxford: Clarendon Press.

Kleingeld, Pauline (2000). "Kantian Patriotism," *Philosophy and Public Affairs,* 29(4), 313–341.

   (2013). *Kant and Cosmopolitanism: The Philosophical Ideal of World Citizenship.* Cambridge: Cambridge University Press.

Loriaux, Sophie (2007). "Kant on International Distributive Justice," *Journal of Global Ethics,* 3(3), 281–301.

O'Neill, Onora (1986). *Faces of Hunger.* London: Allen & Unwin.

   (1996). *Towards Justice and Virtue: A Constructive Account of Practical Reasoning.* Cambridge: Cambridge University Press.

   (2000). *Bounds of Justice.* Cambridge: Cambridge University Press.

   (2016). *Justice across Boundaries.* Cambridge: Cambridge University Press.

Pascoe, Jordan (2015). "Domestic Labor, Citizenship, and Exceptionalism: Rethinking Kant's 'Woman Problem,'" 46(3), 340–356.

Pogge, Thomas (2002). "Is Kant's *Rechtslehre* a 'Comprehensive Liberalism'?" in *Kant's Metaphysics of Morals: Interpretive Essays*, ed. Mark Timmons. Oxford: Oxford University Press, 133–158.

Rawls, John (1971). *A Theory of Justice*. Cambridge, MA: Harvard University Press.

Ripstein, Arthur (2009). *Force and Freedom: Kant's Legal and Political Philosophy*. Cambridge, MA: Cambridge University Press.

Rosen, Allen (1993). *Kant's Theory of Justice*. Ithaca, NY: Cornell University Press.

United Nations Universal Declaration of Human Rights (1950). URL: www.un .org/en/universal-declaration-human-rights/index.html (accessed September 15, 2017).

Varden, Helga (2006). "Kant and Dependency Relations: Kant on the State's Right to Redistribute Resources to Protect the Rights of Dependents," *Dialogue*, 45, 257–284.

Willaschek, Marcus (1997). "Why the *Doctrine of Right* Does Not Belong in the *Metaphysics of Morals*: On Some Basic Distinctions in Kant's Moral Philosophy," *Jahrbuch für Recht und Ethik*, 5, 205–227.

Williams, Howard (2010). "Towards a Kantian Theory of International Distributive Justice," *Kantian Review*, 15(2), 43–77.

  (2012). *Kant and the End of War: A Critique of Just War Theory*. London: Palgrave MacMillan.

Wood, Allen (2008). *Kantian Ethics*. Cambridge: Cambridge University Press.

  (2014). *The Free Development of Each Studies on Freedom, Right, and Ethics in Classical German Philosophy*. New York, NY: Oxford University Press.

Acknowledgments

Many thanks to the series editors and an anonymous referee for tremendously helpful comments, and to students in my spring 2017 graduate seminar on Kant and social welfare for enlightening and thought-provoking discussion.

Cambridge Elements ≡

The Philosophy of Immanuel Kant

Desmond Hogan
Princeton University

Desmond Hogan joined the philosophy department at Princeton in 2004. His interests include Kant, Leibniz and German rationalism, early modern philosophy, and questions about causation and freedom. Recent work includes Kant on Foreknowledge of Contingent Truths, *Res Philosophica* 91 (1) (2014); 'Kant's Theory of Divine and Secondary Causation', in Brandon Look (ed.) *Leibniz and Kant*, Oxford University Press (forthcoming); 'Kant and the Character of Mathematical Inference', in *Kant's Philosophy of Mathematics Vol. I*, Carl Posy and Ofra Rechter (eds.), Cambridge University Press (forthcoming).

Howard Williams
University of Cardiff

Howard Williams was appointed Honorary Distinguished Professor at the Department of Politics and International Relations, University of Cardiff in 2014. He is also Emeritus Professor in Political Theory at the Department of International Politics, Aberystwyth University, a member of the Coleg Cymraeg Cenedlaethol (Welsh-language national college) and a Fellow of the Learned Society of Wales. He is the author of *Marx* (1980); *Kant's Political Philosophy* (1983); *Concepts of Ideology* (1988); *International Relations in Political Theory* (1992); *Hegel, Heraclitus and Marx's Dialectic; International Relations and the Limits of Political Theory* (1996); *Kant's Critique of Hobbes: Sovereignty and Cosmopolitanism* (2003), *Kant and the End of War* (2012) and is currently editor of the journal *Kantian Review.* He is writing a book on the Kantian Legacy in Political Philosophy for a new series edited by Paul Guyer.

Allen Wood
Indiana University

Allen Wood is Ward W. and Pricilla B. Woods Professor at Stanford University. He was a John S. Guggenheim Fellow at the Free University in Berlin, a national Endowment for the Humanities Fellow at the University of Bonn and Isaiah Berlin Visiting Professor at the University of Oxford. He is on the editorial board of eight philosophy journals, five book series and the Stanford Encyclopedia of Philosophy. Along with Paul Guyer, Professor Wood is co-editor of the Cambridge Edition of the Works of Immanuel Kant and translator of the Critique of Pure Reason. He is the author or editor of a number of other works, mainly on Kant, Hegel and Karl Marx. His most recently published book, *Fichte's Ethical Thought*, was published by Oxford University Press in 2016. Wood is a member of the American Academy of Arts and Sciences.

About the Series
This Cambridge Elements series provides an extensive overview of Kant's philosophy and its impact upon philosophy and philosophers. Distinguished Kant specialists will provide an up-to-date summary of the results of current research in their fields and give their own take on what they believe are the most significant debates influencing research, drawing original conclusions.

Cambridge Elements ≡

The Philosophy of Immanuel Kant

Elements in the Series

Kant's Power of Imagination
Rolf-Peter Horstmann
9781108464031

Formulas of the Moral Law
Allen Wood
9781108332736

The Sublime
Melissa McBay Merritt
9781108529709

A full series listing is available at: www.cambridge.org/EPIK